MADRID

POCKET GUIDE

STEAKS

DIAMANT
Restaurant

BROOKLAWN

JOE'S BURGERS

GATE BRIDGE   📍100 m   SHARE

📍 MAP

LIKE

Sailing under the Golden Gate Bridge
today, it is interesting to consider that
engineers once thought it impossible to
span the Golden Gate Strait at this point,
because of the depth of the water (318ft/
97 meters at its deepest point) and the
powerful tidal rush.

The city authorized studies for a bridge
in 1917, but it was 1923 before the first
shovel turned under the gaze of master
engineer Joseph B. Strauss (no relation
to the famous waltz composer). Four
years later the bridge opened, at a cost
of $35 million and the lives of 11
construction workers. Today the bridge

ARTS & CULTURE

Space disco
featuring

A TO Z INFO

SHOPP

Shopping
aroun
be

INSIGHT ⊙ GUIDES

SPAIN

≡   📖 INTRODUCTION

EXPLORE

FLORIDA

This new edition of Insight Guide
Florida is a comprehensive, full-colour
travel guide presents outstanding
photography. Includes everything
from cocktail Taft West and ...

FRANCE

This brand new edition Insight Guide
so full-colour outstanding Insight Guide
full-colour photography, 500 based new
photographs, alive with the places to go
explorations, all all the places to go

T LUCIA Pocket Guide

Walking Eye
mobile app

Discover the world's best destinations with the Insight Guides Walking Eye app, available to download for free in the App Store and Google Play.

The container app provides easy access to fantastic free content on events and activities taking place in your current location or chosen destination, with the possibility of booking, as well as the regularly-updated Insight Guides travel blog: Inspire Me. In addition, you can purchase curated, premium destination guides through the app, which feature local highlights, hotel, bar, restaurant and shopping listings, an A to Z of practical information and more. Or purchase and download Insight Guides eBooks straight to your device.

TOP 10 ATTRACTIONS

PLAZA MAYOR
Take a seat at a terrace café and watch the world go by at the busy centre of local social life. See page 27.

MUSEO NACIONAL CENTRO DE ARTE REINA SOFÍA
A popular showcase of art of the 20th and 21st centuries, including work by Picasso and Luis Buñuel. See page 50.

PUERTA DEL SOL
The plaza's clock tower overlooks the bustling heart of Madrid and chimes in Spain's New Year revelry. See page 36.

EL ESCORIAL
The palace created by Felipe II, where Spain's Golden Age is writ large. See page 70.

THE PRADO

Spain's rich artistic heritage is conserved in one of the world's most prestigious museums. See page 42.

MONASTERIO DE LAS DESCALZAS REALES

A unique chance to see the artistic heritage of a working convent over 450 years. See page 36.

PLAZA SANTA ANA

A great place to start *el tapeo*, the 'tapas crawl'. See page 38.

PALACIO REAL

Elegant centre of royal Madrid. See page 31.

LA ERMITA DE SAN ANTONIO DE LA FLORIDA

Goya's frescoes adorn the cupola of this 18th-century chapel. See page 68.

PARQUE DEL BUEN RETIRO

Its trees, lawns and lake make this Madrid's most child-friendly green space. See page 52.

A PERFECT DAY

9.00am

Santa Ana

Join locals for coffee and fried *churros* as the day gets underway on this classic tree-lined plaza in the city's 18th-century quarter. Don't miss the colourful tiled friezes on bars around the square.

1.00pm

Art and aperitivos

Take a break in the top floor café of Herzog de Meuron's CaixaForum arts centre where you can sip an *aperitivo* and look down on the adjacent vertical garden, a rich tapestry of globally sourced plant varieties.

10.00am

Green oasis

Explore the beautifully tended Real Jardín Botánico where dahlias were first planted in Europe. Three greenhouses are filled with desert and tropical flora and there is an appealing garden gift shop.

11.00am

The Prado

Visit one of the world's greatest art galleries. Do not miss the restored Renaissance Patio de los Jerónimos. The Spanish paintings, largely collected by the royal family, include masterworks by Diego Velázquez and Francisco de Goya.

2.00pm

Classic cocido

Madrid's celebrated chickpea stew, or *cocido*, with its own soup and vegetables, is cooked the old-fashioned way in earthenware pots over charcoal at La Bola, where you lunch with locals at a leisurely pace.

IN MADRID

5.30pm

Shop till you drop
Pedestrianised Calle de Fuencarral, running off Gran Vía, is the city's most fashionable shopping drag. Here you can find hip Spanish fashion brands from Camper shoes to Custo and Hoss Intropia clothes, plus other European fashion. Cafés, bars and ice-cream parlours offer retreats from the street.

10.30pm

Flamenco
Book ahead for the late show at one of the city's *tablaos*, or flamenco clubs, like Casa Patas. Here you will witness an authentic flamenco experience and see artists perform flamenco song, guitar and dance in an intimate and atmospheric environment.

4.00pm

Guernica
Pablo Picasso conceived *Guernica*, one of the 20th century's greatest paintings, as a protest against the Nazi bombing of the Basque village, in 1937. See it hanging alongside his preparatory drawings on the second floor of the Museo Nacional Centro de Arte Reina Sofía.

7.30pm

Tapas time
Enjoy the city's magical dusk light with a *paseo*, or evening stroll, through the sloping old streets that link the Plaza Mayor to the Cava Baja in the medieval old town. Locals end the day there with a glass of fine wine and tapas in coaching inns and designer bars.

CONTENTS

INTRODUCTION

Madrid was little more than a farming town on the arid central plains of Castile when Felipe II plucked it from his royal cap in 1561 and proclaimed it home to the Spanish Court. Ever since then man-made Madrid, which took the reins of Spain's Golden Age, hasn't stopped growing and asserting itself. Though one of Europe's youngest capitals, it's had time and the ambition to rival Spain's more historic cities, including Seville and Valencia. Today it is Spain's political and economic hub, and only Barcelona matches its metropolitan importance.

THE HEART OF SPAIN

Behind Felipe II's royal decree lay a clear logic: Madrid, smack in the centre of Iberia, would promote the monarchy's authority over regional power bases in a newly unified Spain. Today, Madrid is that cohesive centre and more. It is a city to which people have migrated from all over Spain in search of new opportunities; a place where few people claim deep roots.

One step to heaven

'De Madrid al cielo' is a popular saying, which means 'From Madrid, one step to heaven.' As western Europe's highest capital, Madrid boasts spectacular sierra skies and autumn sunsets, captured by Velázquez in his paintings.

Yet at the centre of the modern metropolis, a region of just over 6 million people, its medieval heart lies almost untouched, the alleyways silent at night. For while Spain has leaped forward economically since the 1970s, Madrid is no less characteristically Iberian for that and revels in its traditional way of life. Once, its immigrants were from the Spanish countryside. Today, its newcomers more often come from Latin America and Eastern Europe, but their new customs and fiestas are equally absorbed into the local pattern of life.

Other regions of Spain, such as Catalonia and the Basque country, are more proudly independent in their traditions. Barcelona, Granada and older Castilian court cities possess greater architecture. Many smaller

Taking a break in Plaza Mayor

Spanish cities have finer historic quarters. But *Madrileños* don't begrudge those places anything. Their city may be a planned bureaucrat's town, but its buzzing quality of life keeps Madrid just one rung down from heaven, or so the local saying goes – and many *Madrileños* believe it.

CULTURE AND NIGHTLIFE

In recent years the city has nurtured Spain's most sophisticated cultural life: opera, theatre, *zarzuela* (a form of light comic opera), contemporary dance, jazz and rock, film, circus and graffiti. All have found new audiences here, as has flamenco, Spain's most unique art form.

But Madrid's single greatest cultural draw remains its cluster of superb art museums. On the grand Paseo del Prado are three of Europe's finest: the world-class Museo Nacional del Prado, the Museo Thyssen-Bornemisza and the Museo Nacional Centro de

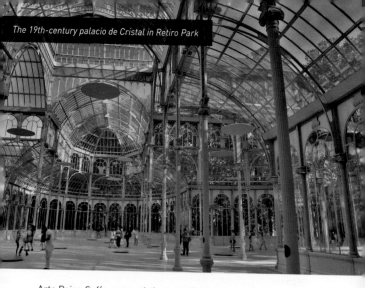

Arte Reina Sofía, currently home to Pablo Picasso's monumental painting, *Guernica*. Madrid's collection of Spanish Old Masters – Velázquez, El Greco, Goya, Zurbarán and more – is unrivalled.

Gregarious at heart, *Madrileños* are night creatures, hopping in and out of *tabernas* (cave-like taverns), restaurants and bars for tapas, Spanish wine and animated conversation until the early hours. The *movida* of the early 1980s, a spontaneous burst of creative nightlife, has given Madrid a name it works hard to maintain. Nightlife still starts and goes on late – very late – with after-hours clubs and bar-hoppers.

GEOGRAPHY

In terms of scale, Madrid's city centre hardly feels like that of a capital city – anyone from London, New York or even Paris is bound to have this impression – and it is easily covered on foot. The city's heart is Old (or Habsburg) Madrid, a largely 16th-century city built around the narrow, winding streets of the earlier Muslim settlement. Its centrepiece is the splendid porticoed Plaza Mayor, rebuilt three times after fires. Nearby are glimpses of the Arab walls, medieval plazas, monasteries and the Palacio Real (Royal Palace), built on the site of the older Muslim Alcázar. The lively Puerta del Sol, still the beating heart of the city, marks the eastern edge of Habsburg Madrid.

The Bourbon monarchs of the 18th century fostered the city's expansion further east. They commissioned grand avenues and boulevards, fountains and gateways. Bourbon Madrid is best symbolised by the handsome Paseo del Prado and the banking mansions between it and the Puerta del Sol. Wedged between this monumental part of town and the historic old town are the city's most characterful popular quarters, such as Lavapiés, Chueca and Malasaña.

Modern Madrid grew unrelentingly in all directions from the early 19th century. Uptown Salamanca is an elegant if faded quarter of apartment buildings and sophisticated shops built around a grid of streets bordered by La Castellana and Paseo de Recoletos, the northward extensions of the Prado boulevard. Both are lined with pavement cafés. Since the 1980s, La Castellana has pushed

⊘ THE CASTIZO SPIRIT

Madrid's flea market, the Rastro, is the mecca of *castizo* culture. Like London's Cockney culture, it is famed for its quick and witty wordplay and its strong community spirit. *Castizo* culture dates back to the 18th century, when the ruling classes began to adopt French styles, and in response the local people developed a swaggering chutzpah and an exaggerated accent deliberately incomprehensible to an outsider.

Cuatro Torres sky scrapers

further north, beyond the financial district. Its northern limit is now marked by Las Cuatro Torres, four spectacular architect-designed towers.

ARCHITECTURE

Madrid's diverse architecture traces the prevailing styles of the different eras in which it spread outwards. Moving from the centre, one passes from stately 16th-century buildings with wrought-iron balconies, brick facades and stone features, to baroque Bourbon palaces, neoclassical buildings and the elegant Belle Epoque, Art Nouveau and Art Deco styles of the Gran Vía. The severe architecture of Franco's dictatorship, on La Castellana, gave way during the 1990s to a wave of eye-catching flagship architecture and, just as important, restoration of the popular old quarters. Their quiet but colourful tree-lined streets are enduringly picturesque.

MODERNITY AND TRADITION

Madrid was at the forefront of the dynamic Spain that emerged after Franco's death in 1975, ending 40 years of dictatorship, cultural and intellectual isolation. Once unshakeably conservative and Catholic, Spain today has one of Europe's lowest birth rates, rapidly falling church attendance and legally recognised gay marriage, while twenty five years of economic boom have been followed by prolonged economic crisis.

What has endured throughout a century of political upheaval and transitions is the love of exuberant street life. After work, *Madrileños* spill on to pavements and into outdoor cafés, those of all ages still take the evening *paseo*, while pensioners play cards or chess in the parks. Come evening, people pack the city's bars.

Madrid clings to *castizo* (working-class *Madrileño*) traditions too. Las Ventas bullring is a shrine for aficionados of bullfighting (*la corrida*) while local *fiestas* such as San Isidro, a celebration of the city's patron saint, are affectionately enjoyed.

'*Nueve meses de invierno y tres de infierno...*' ('Nine months of winter and three of hell...'): the shifts between freezing winters and scorching summers, elegant boulevards and characterful backstreets are marked yet easy ones. There are other contrasts too: Madrid remains a city of *barrios*, or quarters, each of which revels in its own individuality. Traditions are as celebrated as contemporary arts and it is this kaleidoscopic mix which makes the city such a memorable place.

OPTIONS FROM MADRID

Madrid is the perfect base for exploring Castile. A trio of Unesco-honoured cities lie within an hour's journey. Toledo, Spain's former capital, set on a mound above a river moat, keeps an outstanding architectural legacy from its Christian, Jewish and Muslim medieval culture. Segovia, once a royal stronghold, has a fairy-tale castle, a 2,000-year-old aqueduct and wonderful Romanesque churches. The city of Ávila, the birthplace of St Teresa, may be viewed from its perfectly preserved medieval city wall.

Closer to Madrid is the royal monastery of El Escorial, a mausoleum and palace built by Felipe II, from which he governed the Spanish empire. Aranjuez and Chinchón, to the south of Madrid, may be visited together in a day by car. One is an ornamental royal palace and the other a pleasant Castilian country town.

A BRIEF HISTORY

Though prehistoric remains from the Palaeolithic, Neolithic and Bronze Ages have been unearthed in the Manzanares valley, Madrid was just a quiet farming town before its sudden elevation to capital city in 1561.

Over many centuries Madrid's future significance would have been hard to foresee. The Romans dominated and settled large parts of the Iberian peninsula, but left nothing of consequence here. Muslim armies invaded the peninsula in AD 711 via North Africa and overran most of what is Spain today within a decade. It is clear from the Arabic origin of Madrid's name 'place of many springs', variously recorded as Magerit, Mayrit or Magrit, that their appreciation of its endless supply of snow and spring water underlay the growth of the early town.

During three and a half centuries of Muslim rule, the local army built a full-scale fortified palace or *alcázar* on the west-facing heights of Madrid commanding the Manzanares valley. After several unsuccessful skirmishes, the Christian forces of Alfonso VI captured Madrid in 1083, and the *alcázar* became a fort of the crown of Castile. During a counter-offensive in 1109, the town was overrun by Muslims, but the Christianised fortress held and Madrid became a secure walled Christian town. Nonetheless, the Muslim community and

Mudéjar style

Mudéjar architecture refers to a style made popular after the Christian reconquest of Spain. Christians employed Muslim craftsmen to construct buildings with intricate carved and painted Moorish decoration.

Fernando and Isabel greet Christopher Columbus

later its lifestyle continued to be an everyday part of life here long after the fall of Granada in 1492.

Meanwhile, Madrid enjoyed brief prominence in 1309 when Ferdinand IV and his Cortes, an early version of parliament, held a formal meeting in the fledgling town.

Fernando and Isabel, the Catholic monarchs whose marriage united the kingdoms of Aragon and Castile, first visited Madrid in 1477. They appreciated the town's loyalty, but cultured Toledo continued secure in its role as Spain's capital.

SPAIN'S GOLDEN AGE

Under Fernando and Isabel, Spain underwent a dramatic transformation. In 1492 the couple presided over the conquest and discovery of the New World. Over the following century it was to bring great wealth to Spain from the newly established American colonies. Often called the country's Golden Age, this

A public spectacle in the Plaza Mayor, around 1700

was a century of Spanish political supremacy, accompanied by marvels of art and literature, although the roots of decline were present in tensions with the converted Jews and Muslims, economic inflation and the Inquisition's censorship of cultural life.

Fernando and Isabel were consummate Spaniards, committed to the expansion of the crown, closely controlled from an itinerant court. By contrast, their grandson, who assumed the throne as Carlos I in 1516, was born in Flanders in 1500 and could barely express himself in Spanish. The first of the Habsburg dynasty, he packed his retinue with Burgundian and Flemish nobles.

Soon after his arrival in Spain, he inherited the title of Holy Roman Emperor, as Carlos V. His responsibilities in northern Europe kept him busy, away from the royal residences of Toledo, Segovia, Valladolid and Madrid. While the monarch was away, revolts broke out in a number of Spanish cities, including Madrid, where the rebels occupied the *alcázar* (by then a royal palace). The insurrection was quashed and its leaders executed, but the king got the message: he desperately needed to pay more attention to his Spanish subjects.

MADRID'S RISE TO CAPITAL

In 1556, Carlos abdicated in favour of his son, Felipe II – good news for Spain and even better for Madrid. Felipe moved the royal court from Toledo to Madrid in 1561, converting a town of fewer than 15,000 people into the capital of the world's greatest empire. Madrid expanded in a largely improvised way, increasing nearly eight-fold in population in just 50 years. Spain's fortunes as a whole were more volatile. Felipe II took credit for a rousing naval victory at Lepanto against the Turks, but less than two decades later Spain was subjected to the humiliating defeat of its 'invincible' armada, at the hands of Sir Francis Drake. Felipe II's greatest architectural legacy was El Escorial, his severe palace, monastery and library in the foothills of the Sierra de Guadarrama, northwest of Madrid.

Felipe's son, Felipe III was to hold court in Valladolid for several years, though eventually he returned to Madrid. It was he who ordered the construction of the five-storey Plaza Mayor later rebuilt three times. Nearby the 17th-century Plaza de la Villa, little changed today, reveals that Madrid was at last taking itself seriously as a city.

The death of Carlos II, heirless, in 1700 sparked a war over the Spanish succession, which resulted in

Advice unheeded

Felipe II ignored the advice of his father, Carlos I: 'If you wish to conserve your dominions,' he counselled, 'leave the court in Toledo; if you wish to increase them move it to Lisbon; if you do not mind losing them, take it to Madrid.'

the enthronement of the Bourbon Felipe V. When Madrid's *alcázar* burned down in 1734, with the loss of many art treasures, Felipe seized the opportunity to build a lavish new royal palace, today's Palacio Real. The building is still used for government and royal ceremonies, although the royal family lives in the Palacio de la Zarzuela, just to the northwest of Madrid.

Madrid still honours the memory of Carlos III, the most popular Bourbon king, who ruled from 1759 to 1788. He installed public fountains and laid out the Paseo del Prado, he worked hard to pave and lamplight humbler streets and to eradicate crime.

Spain again became a battleground in the early 1800s, with British forces taking on Napoleon's troops in the Peninsular War, called the War of Independence by Spaniards. Napoleon invaded Spain in March 1808 and invested his brother, Joseph, as King José I. On 2 May 1808, Madrid rose up against the interloper. The war went on murderously but inconclusively for six years. Finally, with the help of the British under the Duke of Wellington, the Spanish expelled the occupying forces. In part, Joseph Bonaparte had meant well, he built so many plazas that *Madrileños* nicknamed him *El Rey Plazuelas* – but the people loathed a government imposed from abroad.

DECLINE AND DECADENCE

The son of Carlos IV, Fernando VII, was seated on his right-ful throne in Madrid's Palacio Real in 1814. But the War of Independence and the repercussions of the French Revolution had helped to create in Spain the nucleus of a liberal national-ist party. Power struggles ensued.

The spirit of liberalism prevalent in Europe was tardy in reach-ing Spain. After many reverses, a democratic constitution was finally proclaimed and constitutional monarchy was instituted in 1874. Alongside this, the Spanish–American War of 1898

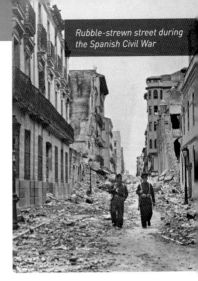
Rubble-strewn street during the Spanish Civil War

marked the final collapse of the Spanish empire of the Golden Age, steadily whittled to insignificance. King Alfonso XIII inaugurated the Madrid Metro and University City, but he was undone by the chronic unrest of his subjects. Neither constitutional government nor dictatorship proved workable, and in 1931 the king went into exile following anti-royalist results in municipal elections.

THE CIVIL WAR

The 1931 general elections created the Second Republic. Bitter ideological conflicts divided parties and produced factions, and the church became heavily involved.

In 1936, a large section of the army under General Francisco Franco rose against the government. On Franco's side (the Nationalists) were monarchists, conservatives, the Catholic Church and the right-wing Falangists. United against him were republicans, liberals, socialists, communists and anarchists. The Civil War developed into one of the great ideological causes of the 20th century. Many Europeans saw the Civil War as a crucial conflict between democracy and dictatorship; or from the other side, as a conflict between law and order and the forces of social revolution and chaos. Madrid remained in Republican hands for most of the war though under siege until March 1939.

War statistics

The Civil War ended with some 700,000 combatants dead; another 30,000 were executed or assassinated; an estimated 15,000 civilians were killed in air raids. Only now are communal tombs being opened.

Hardship, hunger and cultural isolation dogged the 40-year dictatorship following Generalísimo Franco's victory. Although he kept Spain neutral in World War II, some Spaniards enlisted for Hitler, and Nazi planes bombed civilians in the Basque town of Guernica. Finally, Spain was admitted to the United Nations (UN) in 1955 and from the early 1960s, when tourism took off, an economic transformation began that would have profound effects on national identity.

When Franco died in 1975, the coronation of Franco's designated successor, Juan Carlos, the grandson of Alfonso XIII, ushered in the so-called 'transition' to parliamentary democracy. The king's commitment to democracy brought Spain into line with the rest of Western Europe and assured it of future membership in the European Economic Community (now the European Union). In the early 1980s Madrid won a place on the cultural map thanks to its *movida* (see page 12), a street-wise cultural explosion that rejected the stagnation of the Franco era.

MODERN SPAIN

Under Felipe González, Socialist prime minister from 1982 to 1996, Spain stepped onto the world stage. Symbolically, in 1992, Barcelona hosted the Olympic Games, Seville the World Expo, and Madrid was European Capital of Culture. González was credited by many as a principal architect of the new Spain, but his party lost power after incessant charges of corruption. In 1996, José María Aznar formed a conservative (*Partido Popular*) government. During his eight years in power a spectacular property boom began, fuelled by town halls' local control of planning.

On 11 March 2004, three days before national elections, 10 bombs tore through three commuter trains at Atocha station in Madrid. Some 201 people were killed and around 1,500 injured. Aznar's attempt to blame the attack on Basque separatists was one of various factors that created a swing of votes towards the Socialists (PSOE), led by José Luís Zapatero. His reforming spirit in dealing with corruption, ensuring modern civil rights and encouraging a federal state was widely supported, but was dragged down by the government's delayed reaction to the growing economic crisis. By 2011, when elections returned the Partido Popular to power with Mariano Rajoy as prime minister, Spain's unemployment rate was the highest in Europe,

Madrid in 1854, with the old bullring to the fore

and rising. Economic hardships and austerity measures implemented by the government triggered massive social protests, first in Madrid at Puerta del Sol and subsequently in other large cities. The so-called Indignants Movement demanded radical changes in the Spanish politics and turned out to be a springboard for a new anti-establishment left wing party – *Podemos* (meaning "We can").

In 2014 Spain's King Juan Carlos abdicated and his son Felipe VI ascended the throne, with hopes for a new era for the Spanish monarchy. Nevertheless, it was just the beginning of revolutionary changes. A year later, tired of prolonged economic crisis and the corruption scandals ravaging the main political parties (PP and PSOE), the Spaniards let new formations, including *Podemos* and liberal *Ciudadanos*, enter the parliament for the first time.

Later years of Rajoy's tenure were marked by the controversial Catalonia referendum in October 2017, denounced as illegal by the central government. Violent clashes with police, a deepening constitutional crisis and the region's unilateral declaration of independence eventually led to direct rule being imposed from Madrid. Despite widespread international coverage, the Catalan crisis was not nearly as damaging for the government's popularity as the corruption scandal that saw Rajoy lose a vote of no confidence in June 2018. PSOE returned to power with young and energetic economist Pedro Sanchez taking over as prime minister. Sanchez immediately vowed to "reinstate dialogue" with the Catalan independence movement, but the issue remains as thorny as ever. Some 45,000 people took to Madrid's streets in February 2019 to decry what they saw as Sanchez's conciliatory attitude towards Catalonia, as the country prepared for the high-profile trial of twelve of its separatist leaders. Whatever the outcome of the trial, it's certain to provoke impassioned debate about what is already a highly divisive issue in Spain.

HISTORICAL LANDMARKS

900–400 BC Celtic tribes settle and mix with indigenous Iberians.

206 BC End of Carthaginian rule in Spain.

AD 711 Islamic armies invade Spain.

852 Muslims found settlement of Magerit.

996 Madrid conquered by Castile.

1109 Muslims unsuccessfully storm Madrid. Madrid wins town status.

1309 Royal Parliament (Cortes) held in Madrid.

1469 Marriage of Fernando and Isabel unites Aragón and Catalonia with Castile to create a unified Spain.

1492 Moors defeated in Granada; Muslims and Jews expelled.

1561 Felipe II establishes capital in Madrid, replacing Toledo.

1606 Madrid renamed capital of Spain.

1701–13 War of Spanish Succession.

1808–14 Peninsular War; Joseph Bonaparte becomes king.

1874 Restoration of Bourbon monarchy.

1931 Second Republic created after municipal elections.

1936–9 Spanish Civil War ends in Franco dictatorship.

1975 Franco dies, Juan Carlos becomes king.

1986 Spain joins European Community (now European Union).

1992 Madrid is European Capital of Culture.

2004 Ten bombs kill 201 on Madrid commuter trains.

2011 The Indignados (Outraged) occupation of Puerta del Sol in May, in protest at 50 percent youth unemployment, attracts world attention. Partido Popular's Mariano Rajoy becomes PM.

2014 King Juan Carlos abdicates the throne in favour of his son Felipe.

2017 Controversial Catalonian independence referendum is declared illegal by central government in Madrid.

2018 Mariano Rajoy loses vote of no-confidence and is replaced by Pedro Sanchez of PSOE.

2019 High-profile trial of Catalonian separatist leaders begins in Madrid in February. In May, Madrid and 12 other Spanish autonomous communities elect their regional parliaments.

Busy Gran Via

WHERE TO GO

Lying at the heart of the sprawling modern city, the old and new parts of Madrid of greatest interest to visitors are remarkably compact. Old Madrid, the city of the Habsburgs, covers a small area that extends east from the Río Manzanares to Puerta del Sol. Almost all of it can be covered in a day or two, including the lengthy visit to the magnificent Royal Palace. The museums that are home to Spain's great art collections, clustered on the Paseo del Prado, are equally worthy of exploration. For art lovers, the so-called 'Golden Triangle of Art', between central Plaza de Cibeles and Atocha railway station, may be the area where they want to spend most time. Those who enjoy exploring the city's backstreets may like to explore popular old barrios (city quarters) such as Lavapiés, Chueca and Malasaña. Salamanca is more sedate, and Gran Vía is the turn-of-the-20th-century avenue that connects central to western Madrid.

OLD MADRID

Old Madrid, the area spreading outward from the Plaza Mayor, is the city's most historic quarter. After Madrid became the seat of the royal court, this area grew rapidly in the 16th and 17th centuries. Its streets are full of atmospheric *tascas* (bars) and restaurants, churches, aristocratic palaces and major sights like the Palacio Real (Royal Palace), Plaza Mayor, Puerta del Sol and Convento de las Decalzas Reales, Madrid's most important convent.

PLAZA MAYOR

The porticoed **Plaza Mayor ❶**, an architectural symphony of bold but balanced lines, is one of Spain's best-loved squares.

San Miguel Market

Broad arcades surround a cobbled rectangle 200m long and 100m wide (656ft x 328ft). Originally built at the beginning of the 17th century, based on the style of Juan de Herrera (Felipe II's architect, responsible for El Escorial; see page 70), the square we know today, with slate roofs, slender towers and facades of brick and stone dates from 1790–1854. The Plaza Mayor may be entered by any of nine archways. Once it was the scene of pageants, markets, theatre festivals, bullfights, religious processions and even trials and executions during the Spanish Inquisition – residents with access to any of the 400 balconies overlooking the square used to sell tickets for such events. A statue of Felipe III occupies a place of honour, and the Casa de la Panadería (bakery) is decorated with colourful modern frescoes. You can take in the elegant architectural ensemble from a seat at one of the outdoor cafés or during a night-time stroll. A great number of events were held here in 2017 to commemorate the

400th anniversary of the plaza's construction; the square also received a facelift for the occasion.

Leading out of each of the Plaza's arched doorways are narrow, winding streets or stairs. The most famous of these is **Cava San Miguel**, in the southwestern quarter, lined with shops, taverns and *mesones* (cave-like bars). If you head for Calle Mayor on the western side, you'll come first to the **Mercado de San Miguel** (Mon–Thu and Sun 10am–midnight, Fri–Sat 10am–1am; www.mercadodesanmiguel.es), a beautiful Art Nouveau food market, polemically revamped as a pricy emporium for buying and sampling food and wine.

Plaza de la Villa

Further along Calle Mayor is Madrid's oldest square, **Plaza de la Villa ❷**, once the seat of the city's government. The 15th-century Gothic **Casa y Torre de los Lujanes** (House and Tower of the Lujanes) has an imposing stone portal and *mudéjar* tower.

Casa de Cisneros, on the south side of the square, was built in the mid-16th century by a nephew of the inquisitor and warrior, Cardinal Cisneros, and is a fine example of the delicate, ornate style of architecture known as Plateresque. The **Ayuntamiento** (City Hall) dates from the Habsburg era, adorned with the towers and slate spires characteristic of the 17th-century official buildings common in this district of Madrid.

Beyond Calle Mayor, crossing Calle de Bailén, is **Parque Emir Mohammed I**, where you can see fragments of the old Moorish wall that encircled the Magerit settlement.

LA MORERÍA AND LA LATINA

South of Plaza de la Villa and Calle de Segovia is the old Moorish district, **La Morería**, where the intense traffic and bustle of Madrid suddenly subsides. The quiet and pretty square, **Plaza de la Paja** (Straw Square), was the commercial focus of the city in the days before the Plaza Mayor. On the south side of the plaza, with its entrance around the other side, is **Iglesia de San Andrés**, splendidly restored (daily 9am–1pm, 6–8pm, Sun 9am–1pm; free). Inside is the **Capilla del Obispo**, marking the original burial place of Madrid's patron saint.

Adjoining it is the **Museo de San Isidro**, also known as **Museo de los Orígenes de Madrid ❸** (Plaza de San Andrés; Tue–Sun 10am–8pm, mid-June–mid-Sept until 7pm; free), built within the restored shell of the palace of the Vargas family, for whom Isidro worked as a labourer. Built around a large patio planted with local sierra trees and flowers, the museum gives a lively overview of Madrid when it was a farming town, using fossils, 3D audiovisuals, artefacts and architectural models.

Iglesia de San Andrés

Just southwest of here is the formidable mid-18th-century **Real Basílica de San Francisco el Grande ❹** (Basilica of St Francis of Assisi; Tue–Sat 10.30am–12.30pm and 4–6pm, July–Sept Tue–Sun 10.30am–12.30pm and 5–7pm). When Madrid's most important friary was rebuilt in neoclassical style, a dome was added with an inner diameter of more than 31m (100ft), larger than that of the cupola of St Paul's in London. The church's paintings include works by Goya, Ribera and Zurburán.

East of Plaza, San Andrés is a closely packed network of animated alleys and streets: among them, **Cava Baja**, **Cava Alta** ❺, Calle Almendro and Calle del Nuncio. They are home to craft shops and, increasingly, bars or eateries inside old taverns. The barrio was one of Madrid's classic working-class areas and is at its most lively on Sunday mornings when **El Rastro** fleamarket (see page 90) fills a warren of streets entered from Calle de Toledo, a lively thoroughfare that leads back up to the Plaza Mayor.

El Rastro fleamarket

On Calle de Toledo stands the **Colegiata de San Isidro** (daily 7.30am–1pm and 6–9pm; free). Built by the Jesuits in the early 17th century, this church was modelled on that of the Gesu in Rome, and between 1885 and 1993, was Madrid's cathedral. It remains so today in many *Madrileños'* hearts. San Isidro keeps many relics, including the revered remains of the city's patron saint, San Isidro Labrador, and a Virgin wearing a military sash awarded by Franco.

PALACIO REAL

The **Palacio Real** ❻ (Royal Palace; daily 10am–6pm, Apr–Sept until 8pm; free for EU citizens last two hours Mon–Thu; www.patrimonionacional.es), just west of the Plaza de Oriente, was built in the 18th century on the site of the medieval wooden *alcázar* destroyed by fire in 1734. The new grey stone palace, commissioned by Bourbon king Felipe V, was completed in 1755. Set among formal gardens on a bluff overlooking the Manzanares valley, this imperious residence is loaded with art and history.

Guided and self-guided tours of the palace take in only a fraction of the 2,000 rooms (more than any other palace in Europe), but many of its highlights. You can also see the formal Changing of the Royal Guard on the first Wednesday of every month at noon (excluding Aug–Sept and during bad weather). The first feature visitors see is the immense **Plaza de la Armería**, which overlooks the valley west of Madrid. The entrance to the palace is via the main staircase – bright, airy and ceremonious beneath an arched ceiling. Each step is a single slab of marble. The

The Palacio Real

Salón de los Halberdiers contains remarkably well-preserved ancient Flemish and Spanish tapestries. The walls of the **Salón del Trono** (Thron e Room) are covered by red velvet and mirrors in matching gilt frames. Its ceiling was painted by Tiepolo in 1764. The conversation antechamber, contributed by Carlos III, has four handsome portraits by Goya.

Royal guards on parade

The apartments of Carlos III consist of one lavish room after another. The outstanding **Salón de Gasparini** is named after the artist, Matias Gasparini of Naples, who mobilised stonecutters, sculptors, glass-blowers, clockmakers, silversmiths, cabinet-makers and embroiderers to produce this stunning example of the rococo style, in which floor, walls and ceiling swirl with special effects. The **Sala de Porcelana** (Porcelain Room) is an almost-overwhelming display of porcelain, incorporating over 1,000 18th-century pieces from the factory that then stood in the Retiro Park.

The regal, extravagant **Comedor de Gala** (Ceremonial Dining Room), built for the wedding of Alfonso XII and his second wife, María Cristina, in 1879, seats 145 guests. Notice the 15 chandeliers, 10 candelabra and 18th-century Chinese porcelain jars along walls hung with Brussels tapestries.

Two highlights for many visitors are the early Hapsburg **Botica Real** (Royal Pharmacy) and **Armería Real** (Royal

Armoury). Built in 1594, the pharmacy's cupboards line two rooms with matching glass-and-porcelain apothecary jars. The Armería Real (Royal Armoury) displays authentic battle flags, trophies, shields and weapons, a collection regarded as one of the finest of its type in the world. In warm weather leave time for a stroll around the royal gardens: the formal **Jardines de Sabitini** and wooded **Campo del Moro** (entrance Paseo Virgen del Puerto, opening hours as for the Palacio Real).

ALMUDENA CATHEDRAL

Adjacent to the palace is the **Catedral de Nuestra Señora de la Almudena** (daily 9am–8.30pm; closed during mass; www. catedraldelaalmudena.es), which was finished in 1993 more than 350 years after the cornerstone was laid. The cathedral is constructed on the site of Muslim Magerit, but its most historic surviving feature is the 16th-century image of the Virgen de la Almudena, patroness of Madrid, which is kept in the crypt. Guided tours (Mon–Sat 10am–2.30pm) include the climb up to the dome.

⊙ DRAMA AT THE OPERA

The Teatro Real has had a chequered past. Built on the site of the Plaza de Oriente's wash house, it opened with a performance of Donizetti's *La Favorita* in 1850, on the birthday of Queen Isabel II, who was an opera fanatic. However, it was closed only 75 years later, when it was found that the stream running beneath it had brought its foundations to the point of collapse. Used as a gunpowder arsenal during the Civil War, the theatre was left closed during Franco's regime – he disliked opera – until it re-opened as a concert hall in 1965. It finally re-opened again, after a decade-long and extravagantly budgeted restoration, in 1999.

In May 2004, the cathedral hosted its first royal wedding, that of Prince Felipe of Asturias and former journalist Letizia Ortiz.

PLAZA DE ORIENTE AND OPERA

The Royal Palace's front facade overlooks the stately **Plaza de Oriente**, lined with statues of Spanish kings and queens, and the **Teatro Real ❼**, Madrid's opera house. A guided visit

Inside the cathedral

(daily; www.teatro-real.com) takes in the Teatro's opulent salons and the auditorium which was built over a small river, giving excellent acoustics, but construction problems. Behind the opera house in Plaza Isabel II, underground inside the Metro station, you can see the excavated aqueduct, channelling and wash house fed by the river.

A couple of blocks away stands the **Real Monasterio de la Encarnación ❽** (Convent of the Incarnation; opening hours see: Monasterio de las Descalzas Reales), on the small plaza of the same name. Founded in 1611 by Margarita de Austria, this convent's most fascinating feature is the reliquary room, containing saints' bones and other body parts in gilded cabinets. A small phial of San Pantaleón's blood kept there mysteriously liquefies on the afternoon of 26 July every year. In the 18th-century church, you may hear the nuns pray or sing, but you'll never see them; they are cloistered behind the grillwork.

Nearby is the **Monasterio de las Descalzas Reales** ❾ (Royal Barefoot Franciscans; Tue–Sat 10am–2pm and 4–6.30pm, Sun and hols 10am–3pm, free Wed and Thu pm for EU citizens, guided tour only; joint ticket available with the Convento de la Encarnación; www.patrimonionacional.es). Founded by Princess Juana de Austria, the daughter of Carlos V, in 1566, this palace was transformed into a convent by the architect responsible for El Escorial. The convent, supported by wealthy patrons, accepted only nuns of the highest nobility until the beginning of the 18th century. The sisters brought with them spectacular works of art set aside originally as their marriage dowries. Until 30 years ago, the convent was completely cloistered and no visits allowed. Today, Franciscan nuns – a maximum of 33 (the age of Jesus when he died) – remain on the premises, but stay out of sight during visiting hours.

The convent's finest feature is its theatrical granite stairway, splashed with splendid 17th-century frescoes from floor to ceiling. On the second floor are rooms with heavy timbered ceilings whose walls are covered with works of art, mostly of religious or royal significance. In one hall hang a dozen splendid 17th-century tapestries based on original Rubens drawings. The museum also contains outstanding paintings by Titian, Brueghel the Elder and Zurbarán, fleetingly pointed out as you pass through the galleries.

Churches galore

There are more than 200 churches in Madrid. In the Spanish context they are relatively modern, but include fine examples of Mudéjar and Baroque work.

PUERTA DEL SOL

Plaza Puerta del Sol ❿ is Madrid's busiest plaza and for centuries has been the heart of the city. It also marks the transition between Habsburg Madrid and the city laid out by the Bourbon

Puerta del Sol and the Casa de Correos

kings. The original gate that once existed here – originally the eastern gate of the Muslim town – was torn down in 1570. Ten streets converge on the plaza. 'Kilometre Zero', a metal plaque set into the pavement below the clock tower, is the point from which distances from Madrid in Spain and Latin America are measured.

The neoclassical brick building below the clock tower, the **Casa de Correos** dating from 1768, houses the regional government. Thousands of *Madrileños* gather here for a New Year's Eve ritual. They each swallow a dozen grapes while the clock atop the building strikes midnight, a ritual said to bring good luck for the coming year.

Almost lost in the bustle of the Puerta del Sol is a small statue based on Madrid's coat of arms, which depicts a bear leaning against a *madroño* tree (an arbutus, or strawberry tree). The bear is a symbol of Madrid, and the strawberry tree one of the sierra's most distinctive plants. Whatever time of day you visit this hectic

Plaza, you will find it buzzing not only with visitors, but also, often, buskers and locals sharing news and views. Since the occupation of the plaza by young Spanish *Indignados* in 2011 it has become a symbol of the 15M Movement (see page 23).

HUERTAS AND SANTA ANA

Southeast of Puerta del Sol lie **Plaza Santa Ana** and Calle de las Huertas, both today lined with restaurants and bars. Once the area had bullfighting associations: bullfighter Manolete was a regular at the Reina Victoria hotel, now the Me Hotel, on Plaza Santa Ana. The square itself is named after the convent that stood here till it disappeared in the 1830s. Also on the square, on the site of an earlier open-air *corral*, is the historic **Teatro Español** (http://teatroespanol.es), while at Plaza Santa Ana 6 is Cervecería Alemana (www.cerveceriaalemana.com), where writers Ernest Hemingway and Lillian Hellman used to hang out.

Reached off the southern side of Plaza Santa Ana, **Calle de las Huertas**, now pedestrianised, has literary quotes set into paving stones in honour of the great authors of the Golden Age and later periods, who lived here close to the theatres where their plays were performed. Not far away, you

Bear and strawberry tree, symbol of Madrid, in Puerta del Sol

Facades in Lavapiés

can visit the **Casa Museo Lope de Vega** ⑪ (Calle Cervantes 11; Tue–Sun 10am–6pm; only guided tours, book ahead; free; http://casamuseolopedevega.org). The home of Spain's most famous dramatist is beautifully restored as a museum of 17th-century life.

LAVAPIÉS

South of Plaza Santa Ana and Antón Martín Metro station is the sloping quarter of **Lavapiés** (literally 'wash feet'), legendarily named after a fountain used for washing feet. In the 15th century, this was the old Jewish quarter, which has left its mark in winding and twisting streets, the remains of a synagogue under the church of San Lorenzo, and the saintly Catholic street names given when the Jews were expelled. Still one of Madrid's most lively working-class districts, this quarter is now home to a thriving alternative arts scene.

At the heart of the area is lively **Plaza de Lavapiés**. All around the square and in the streets running off it are interesting bars and restaurants. There are excellent Arab cafés and an increasing selection of Indian and Turkish ones – but older locals remain loyal to their traditional Spanish roots and tend to favour dishes such as *cocido*, Madrid's one-pot chickpea stew, *caracoles* (snails), *callos* (tripe) and *oreja* (fried strips of pig's ear).

On the eastern side of Lavapiés spreads **El Rastro**, Madrid's famous Sunday flea market.

CALLE DE ALCALÁ TO PLAZA DE CIBELES

East of Puerta del Sol are the city's 18th-century quarters engineered by the Bourbon monarchs. **Calle de Alcalá**, once the city's main financial district, leads to the Plaza de Cibeles and the Paseo del Prado. Its spacious boulevards, grand plazas and fountains are interspersed with imposing 18th-century blocks that house the head offices or branches of more than 100 banks, plus insurance companies, and, on nearby Plaza de la Lealtad, the Bolsa de Comercio (Stock Exchange).

On Calle de Alcalá is the **Real Academia de Bellas Artes de San Fernando** ⑫ (museum Tue–Sun and hols 10am–3pm, closed Aug; free on Wed and National hols; www.realacademiabellasartessanfernando.com) – the Royal Academy, home to a celebrated collection of Goya's paintings, including *Burial of the Sardine*, and a superb self-portrait of the artist in his old age. Works by Velázquez, Murillo and Rubens are also represented along with a magnificent collection of paintings by Zurbarán, rivalling that of the Prado.

Just before the junction of Calle de Alcalá with the Paseo del Prado sits the **Círculo de Bellas Artes** ⑬, a cultural centre (entrance Calle Marqués de Casa Riera 2; exhibitions Tue–Sun 11am–2pm, 5–9pm; www.circulobellasartes.com), which was

The goddess and her chariot on Plaza de Cibeles

built in 1927. The centre's café (Mon–Thu 8am–1am; Fri–Sun until 3am; free entrance), replete with chandeliers, vast windows and a grand marble nude by Moisés Huerta (1910), is a favourite among the city's cultural crowd.

The entrance fee includes a visit to the rooftop Azotea (Mon–Fri 9am–9pm, Sat–Sun 11am–9pm) for spectacular 365-degree views from the seventh floor.

The point where Calle Alcalá crosses the old city's main north-south artery is a huge, noisy and polluted – yet still impressive – crossroads called **Plaza de Cibeles**. The central fountain shows Cybele, the Greek goddess of fertility and symbol of the city, serenely settled in a chariot pulled by two lions. On the south-eastern side, the **Palacio de Comunicaciones** (Tue–Sun 10am–8pm), inaugurated in 1919 as one of Europe's grandest post offices, has been revamped as the city hall. Located on the south-west corner of Plaza de Cibeles is the **Banco de España** (Bank of Spain) and on the northeast corner is the **Casa de America**, a Latin American cultural centre housed in the plush 19th-century **Palacio de Linares** ⓮ (Sat–Sun guided tours at 11am, noon and 1pm; www.casaamerica.es).

PASEO DEL PRADO

The elegant **Paseo del Prado**, the southern kilometre of the great 5km (3-mile) long Paseo de la Castellana, is home to one of the world's most impressive cluster of art museums: the Prado, the Thyssen Bornemisza, the Reina Sofía and the smaller CaixaForum. Visitors can stroll down the Paseo's shady boulevard, designed for carriages, head to the Botanical Garden or explore smaller nearby museums.

MUSEO DEL PRADO

The **Museo Nacional del Prado** ⓯ (Mon–Sat 10am–8pm, Sun and hols until 7pm; free last two hours; advanced booking tel: 902-107 077; www.museodelprado.es) houses one of the world's largest and most prestigious painting collections. In November 2019, the museum will celebrate its 200th anniversary. Apart from its Spanish treasures, it includes great works from both the Italian and Flemish schools. The immense collection, ranging from the 12th–19th century, was collected and commissioned by Spain's Habsburg and Bourbon kings, private patrons, and convents and monasteries around the country.

Despite its greatness, the museum came about somewhat by chance. In the 18th century, Carlos III commissioned the architect Juan de Villanueva, draughtsman of the royal palace, to design this neoclassical building as a museum of natural history next to a botanical garden. After some eventful delays (Napoleon's invasion badly damaged the building), it was decided to use it instead for art. It was inaugurated in 1819 and in 1868 it became El Museo del Prado.

Modernisation work in 2007 added a new wing for temporary shows. Pritzker prize-winning Spanish architect Rafael Moneo designed the extension in the former cloisters of the neighbouring Jeronimite church opposite, with splendid contemporary wrought iron doors by Basque artist Cristina Iglesias.

Inside the Prado

The nearby Casón del Buen Retiro, which used to house later 19th-century paintings (and later Picasso's *Guernica*, at his own request for it to hang in the Prado), is now the museum's study centre and one of the best libraries.

The Prado owns around 8,600 paintings, but at present can only display about 2,000 of them (the overflow is either in storage or on loan to museums around Spain and elsewhere). The result is a stunning collection of master works considered unique primarily for the Habsburgs' collecting tastes, which were unusually broad for the period, cutting across nationalities and cultures.

Visitors often opt for condensed highlights – the illustrated guide sheet facilitates this – and so artworks here are ordered by nationality of schools rather than as a comprehensive tour of the museum.

Highlights of the Prado

SPANISH: The greatest Spanish artist of the Golden Age, **Diego Velázquez y Silva** (1599–1660) was hired by King Felipe IV and became an amazingly perceptive court painter and portraitist. The Prado keeps nearly three-quarters of his paintings. The royal family is featured in his seminal work, **Las Meninas** (*The Maids of Honour*). The artist painted himself, palette in hand, at the side of his own masterpiece, in a sense part of the family.

Another vast, unforgettable canvas here is *Surrender of Breda*, commemorating a Spanish victory over Dutch forces in 1625. Chivalry and exhaustion, the array of upraised lances, and the burning landscape communicate a profound pathos, as does his study of Mars, the god of war, hanging close by. Other great works include *Las Hilanderas* (*The Spinners*) and *Los Borrachos* (*The Drunkards*).

Diego de Acedo (1644), by Velázquez, in the Prado

Francisco de Goya (1746–1828), another great court painter, had a tumultuous, wildly varied career. His works in the Prado, which trace an extraordinary lifelong evolution of style, form the largest Goya ensemble in the world. Born in Aragon, Goya fled Zaragoza in 1763 for the anonymity of Madrid where he went on to become the king's principal artist. Among the Prado's paintings is **La Maja Desnuda** (*The Naked*

Goya's 'La Maja Desnuda', radically modern when first revealed

Maja), one of Spain's first nudes. Rumours of a scandalous affair between Goya and the Duchess of Alba have long been assumed though art historians now suggest the *maja* – a *Madrileño* name for an attractive woman – was Spanish politician Godoy's lover. Goya's most celebrated royal portrait, *The Family of Carlos IV* is daringly honest; only the royal children look remotely attractive. On another level his large canvas, **The Executions of the 3rd of May**, one of history's most powerful protest pictures, depicts the shooting of Spanish patriots by the French in 1808. Goya witnessed this tragedy of the War of Independence from his cottage, and went to the scene to sketch the victims by moonlight. His most mature harrowing 'black paintings', done at home, in old age, when he is said to have lost his sanity *(see Saturn Devouring One of His Sons)*, are extraordinarily modern in conception and form a focal point in a dramatically lit gallery.

El Greco (1541–1614), born in Crete and long a resident in Italy, became a consummate Spanish painter. He worked in Toledo, his adopted city, for 37 years, toiling at the immense, intensely personal, religious canvases, typically in blacks, yellows and deep mauves, with elongated figures that are his hallmark. *Knight with His Hand on Chest*, an early portrait, is a study of a deep-eyed caballero (gentleman) in black. It is signed, in Greek letters, 'Domenikos Theotokopoulos', the artist's real name. The Prado also has several of El Greco's passionately coloured religious paintings, such as *Adoration of the Shepherds*.

Francisco de Zurbarán (1598–1664), a friar and member of the Seville school, combined mysticism and realism. His greatest works are of mythological, religious and historic themes. Monks, priests and saints are portrayed in flowing robes with almost tangible textures. The Prado owns his strained but fascinating battle picture *The Defence of Cádiz Against the English* and his *Still Life*, of a goblet, two vases and a pot emerging from a black background.

Bartolomé Murillo (1617–82), Spain's most popular religious artist of his time, depicted Biblical personalities at ease. His tender and classical religious works brought him international fame, although detractors label his work mawkish.

José Ribera (c.1591–1652) spent much of his life in Italy, where the Valencia-born artist was known as *lo Spagnoletto* (the little Spaniard). His portraits of saints, hermits and martyrs reveal impeccable drawing skills, composition and keen awareness of the power of light and shadow.

Optical defect

In the 20th century, some critics wondered whether El Greco's revolutionary elongated figures were the result of astigmatism.

DUTCH, FLEMISH AND GERMAN: Hieronymus

Bosch's 'The Garden of Earthly Delights'

Bosch (c.1450–1516), whom the Spanish call *El Bosco*, has three masterpieces in the Prado, including the large, extraordinarily detailed triptych **The Garden of Earthly Delights**. Daringly mixing erotic fantasies and apocalyptic nightmares, it portrays the terrors and superstitions of the medieval peasant mind. Bosch's wild hallucinations presage similar psychological explorations 400 years later by Salvador Dalí.

Peter Paul Rubens (1577–1640) pursued a career as a diplomat as well as an artist. Of particular note is his huge *Adoration of the Magi*, a brilliant religious extravaganza, and *The Three Graces*, a portrait of fleshy nudes; the woman on the right is said to be Rubens' second wife, Helena.

The finest work of **Rogier van der Weyden** (c.1400–64), the altarpiece *Descent From the Cross*, is on the ground floor. Elsewhere is a famous work by German Renaissance painter **Albrecht Dürer** (1471–1528) – his **Self-Portrait at 26.**

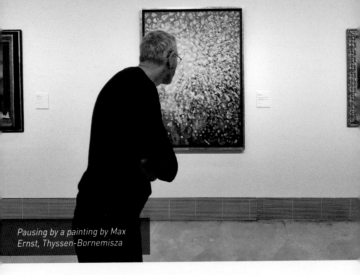

ITALIAN: works by **Titian** (c.1490–1576) include the *Portrait of the Emperor Carlos V*. Depicting Titian's patron in armour, on horseback at the Battle of Mühlberg, it set the standard for court painters for the next century. Titian also produced religious works, but seemed to have no difficulty changing gears to the downright lascivious, as in his *Baccanal*.

The collection of paintings by **Raphaël** (1483–1520) in the Prado was at one point taken lock, stock and barrel to Paris under the orders of Napoleon, but it was soon returned. Centuries of investigation have failed to uncover the identity of *The Cardinal*, Raphael's explosive character study of a subject with fish-like eyes, aquiline nose and cool, thin lips.

Tintoretto (1518–94) brought Mannerism to Venice. Look for his representations of dramatic biblical stories and, on quite another plane, the close-up of a *Lady Revealing her Bosom*.

If you need respite from the vast museum, pop into the neighbouring Jardín Botánico, or head toward Calle Huertas for everyday street life and refreshments.

MUSEO THYSSEN-BORNEMISZA

On the opposite side of the Paseo del Prado, in the salmon-coloured Palacio de Villahermosa, is the **Museo Thyssen-Bornemisza ⑯** (Paseo del Prado 8; Mon noon–4pm, Tue–Sun 10am–7pm, free permanent exhibition on Mon; www.museothyssen.org). The Thyssen Collection, widely considered to be the greatest private collection after that of England's Queen Elizabeth II, opened in Madrid in 1992. Previously, it hung in Baron Thyssen-Bornemisza's Villa Favorita, at Lugano. His wife Baroness Carmen's impressive personal collection is housed in an extension of the museum.

What makes the collection so interesting is the personal 'eye' behind the 800 paintings on display, dating from the 13th century to the present day. From the 19th and 20th centuries there are carefully chosen examples of work from key movements: the Paris school, German expressionism, Russian avant-garde and 19th-century American painting. Among the classical works are stunning paintings by Fra Angélico, Van Eyck, Dürer, Rembrandt, Hals, Titian, Van Dyck and Rubens. The Impressionists are represented by Manet, Monet, Renoir, Gauguin, Toulouse-Lautrec, Cézanne and Van Gogh.

The representation of artists from the second half of the 20th century to the present day includes works by Francis Bacon (*Portrait of George Dyer in a Mirror*, 1968), Robert Rauschenberg, David Hockney, Lucian Freud, Roy Lichtenstein and other pop artists.

MUSEO NACIONAL CENTRO DE ARTE REINA SOFÍA

Among the cluster of museums on the Paseo del Prado, the **Museo Nacional Centro de Arte Reina Sofía** ⓱ (Calle de Santa Isabel 52; Mon and Wed–Sat 10am–9pm, Sun and hols 10am–7pm; free Mon, Wed–Sat after 7pm, Sun after 1.30pm; www.museoreinasofia.es), is the fastest-growing collection. Housed in an 18th-century hospital, it currently shows its modern art collection in chronological sections, interweaving work by Spanish and non-Spanish artists and ranging from the turn of the 20th century up to the present. The most celebrated work on show is Picasso's monumental *Guernica*, which is displayed behind bulletproof glass. The centre also houses works by Miró,

⊙ GUERNICA

Painted in 1937, at the height of the Spanish Civil War, Picasso's *Guernica* was commissioned for the Spanish pavilion of the World's Fair in Paris by Luis Buñuel. In April of that year the Luftwaffe, intervening on behalf of Franco, bombed the town of Guernica (Gernika) in the heart of Spain's Basque region, targeting civilians. Rather than dwelling on the political implications, Picasso directed his intense focus on the suffering caused by violence. Blending techniques from cubism and surrealism, he composed a work of enigmatic yet powerful allusions to earlier Iberian and Spanish art. During and after World War II, the painting came to be seen as a universal expression of anti-war sentiment, and it has also served as a banner for the Basque independence movement. Picasso, who died in 1973, bequeathed the painting to Spain, but stipulated that the legacy should only take effect when democracy was re-established. It was finally brought to Madrid in 1981 after Spain discarded dictatorship.

Admiring Picasso's 'Guernica' in the Centro de Arte Reina Sofía

Dalí, Julio González, Juan Gris and Luis Buñuel, and hosts temporary exhibitions. A modern addition, Edificio Nouvel, has two temporary exhibition spaces, library, café and two concert halls.

ATOCHA

Directly across from the Reina Sofía is the **Estación de Atocha**, a lofty iron-and-glass hangar-like affair modelled on London's St Pancras station, occupied by a tropical garden. In March 2004 Atocha was catapulted into the world news following bomb attacks on suburban trains by Al-Qaeda. In the wake of the bombings Atocha's local station became a shrine of church candles with messages to the bombs' victims. Today the station keeps an underground monument in which visitors gaze skywards through a giant perspex cylinder engraved with some of the messages left here in 2004 (Tue–Sun 11am–2pm, 5–7pm; free).

OTHER MUSEUMS

Smaller museums in the vicinity of the Prado include **CaixaForum** ⑱ arts centre housed in an old brick power station (Paseo del Prado 36; daily 10am–8pm). Converted by Herzog and de Meuron, this intriguing geometric brick building stands alongside a 24m (78ft) vertical wall-garden planted with tropical vegetation. Southeast of Atocha is the **Real Fábrica de Tapices** ⑲ (Royal Tapestry Factory; Calle Fuentarrabía 2; Mon–Fri 10am–2pm, guided visits only; www.realfabrica detapices.com), which still works with most of the original 18th-century machinery. Finally, close to Plaza de Cibeles, the **Museo Nacional de Artes Decorativas** ⑳ (National Museum of Decorative Arts; Tue–Sat 9.30am–3pm, Sun and hols 10am–3pm, Sept–June Thu also 5–8pm; free Sun, hols and Thu pm; www.culturaydeporte.gob.es/mnartesdecorativas) is a fine collection which includes a spectacular tiled 18th-century Valencian kitchen on the top floor.

PARQUE DEL RETIRO

East of the museums is the city centre's major green space, **Parque del Buen Retiro** (daily 6am–10pm, May–Sept until midnight). Until 1868, the park was a royal preserve. Today it is a favourite place for *Madrileños* to stroll or relax in the sun. The rowing boats (10am–8pm or sunset if earlier; charge for 45 min sessions) on **El Estanque**, the park's small central lake, are a big attraction all year round. On the eastern side of the lake a semicircular stone colonnade makes a majestic backdrop to a bronze **monument to Alfonso XII**, unveiled by his son, Alfonso XIII. The latter survived a bomb attack on the day of his wedding to Queen Victoria's granddaughter, Victoria Eugenia, grandmother of today's King Juan Carlos, thanks to a message carved on a tree in the Retiro.

Boating on the lake, Parque del Retiro

Other highlights within the park include the **Palacio de Cristal** ㉑ (Crystal Palace; daily 10am–6pm, Oct until 7pm, Apr–Sept until 10pm; free; www.museoreinasofia.es), a jewel-like 19th-century greenhouse modelled on London's Crystal Palace, that now houses contemporary art exhibitions; the rose garden, **La Rosaleda**, where the old varieties of roses smell as lovely as they look (the best time to visit is April to June). In the southwest area of the park, the only public statue in Europe dedicated to the devil, **El Angel Caído** *(The Fallen Angel)*, depicts the expulsion of the fallen angel, Lucifer, from the Garden of Eden – a neo-Baroque rendering by the sculptor Ricardo Bellver (1885).

REAL JARDÍN BOTÁNICO

A quieter green oasis, next to the Prado, is the **Real Jardín Botánico** ㉒ (Royal Botanical Garden; Plaza de Murillo 2; daily

Parque del Retiro's Palacio de Cristal

10am–dusk, Nov–Feb until 6pm, May–Aug until 9pm; www.rjb.csic.es). It was founded 250 years ago and is laid out around centennial trees, fascinating flowers and rare species. The first dahlias in Europe originated here from seeds brought back from Mexico. In 1803, 7,000 packets of dahlia seeds were sent from here to England, France and Italy for propagation.

At the northwest corner of the Retiro is **Puerta de Alcalá**, a monumental triumphal arch surmounted by warrior-angels, honouring Carlos III. Until the late 19th century, this marked the eastern edge of Madrid. Now called the Plaza de la Independencia, the arch or gateway has become a decorative symbol of the city's cultural openness, seen as a monument to its cosmopolitan tolerance.

RECOLETOS AND CASTELLANA

The **Paseo de Recoletos**, a 19th-century prolongation of the Paseo del Prado, runs from Plaza de Cibeles to Plaza Colón, where it becomes the **Paseo de la Castellana**, Madrid's principal north–south avenue, running up to the city's northern limits. Patrician townhouses and palaces give way to ministry buildings from Franco's period, modern apartment blocks and high-rise offices. Several notable museums are housed in this quarter.

AROUND THE PASEO DE RECOLETOS

On the eastern side of the Paseo de Recoletos stands the completely restored **Museo Arqueológico Nacional** ㉓ (National Archaeological Museum; Calle de Serrano 13; Tue–Sat 9.30am–8pm, Sun and hols 9.30am–3pm; free Sat after 2pm and Sun; www.man.es). The museum's collection of art and artefacts stretches from Spain's ancient cultures – Greek, Roman and Visigothic – to the Romanesque pilgrimage route. One star exhibit is the *Dama de Elche*, a stone sculpture found in Alicante province in 1897 and thought to be 2,500 years old.

Outside the museum's front door is an intriguing underground reproduction of the painted prehistoric scenes discovered in a cave in Altamira in northern Spain.

Museo Arqueológico

Museo Sorolla paintings

Recoletos has distinct moods by day and night. Calm during the day, on summer nights its *terrazas* – open-air terrace bars – cater for an elegant well-heeled crowd into the early hours. Among the *terrazas* on the Paseo's west side are the quaint retro kiosks of the traditional **Café Gijón** (No. 21; www.cafegijon.com), an intellectuals' and artists' haunt for over a century; and atmospheric **Café Espejo** (No. 31; www.restauranteelespejo.com). Both stay open all year round.

COLÓN

Plaza de Colón is a large open space where skateboarders gather to practise among hurried businessmen and pram-pushing mothers. An 1885 statue of Christopher Columbus overlooks a larger modern stone monument to the discovery of the New World. Under the square is the **Centro Cultural de la Villa** (City Cultural Centre) where the Teatro Fernán Gómez hosts seasons of jazz, gospel, flamenco and theatre.

ALONG THE CASTELLANA

About six blocks north and slightly east is the charming **Museo Sorolla** 24 (Paseo del General Martínez Campos 37; Tue–Sat 9.30am–8pm, Sun 10am–3pm; free Sat from 2pm and Sun; www.culturaydeporte.gob.es/msorolla). This mansion was the home and studio of Joaquín Sorolla (1863–1923), the Valencian Impressionist painter. It now displays 300 of his light-filled seaside scenes and landscapes and preserves a small lovingly tended garden.

Back on the Castellana, around five minutes' walk further north, are the ornate domes of the **Museo de Ciencias Naturales** ㉕ (Natural Science Museum; entrance off Calle de José Gutiérrez Abascal 2; Tue–Fri 10am–5pm, Sat–Sun 10am–8pm, July–Aug daily 10am–5pm; www.mncn.csic.es). The museum is home to giant skeletons and dinosaur replicas as well as interactive, child-orientated displays on the animal kingdom, anthropological and mineral collections.

SALAMANCA

Salamanca, Madrid's most sedate city quarter, lies east of the Castellana. It came into existence in the mid-1880s when the city's growing population made it necessary to expand beyond the old city centre. At its heart, presiding over the junction of Calles Príncipe de Vergara and Ortega y Gasset, and in the plaza that bears his name, is a statue of the character responsible for building the quarter, the Marqués de Salamanca (1806–83), José or 'Pepito' to his friends. A financier, politician, lawyer and patron of the arts, his career, a roller-coaster of fortunes made and lost, ended in ruin in 1867.

The Bernabéu

About half way out along the Castellana is the famous Santiago Bernabéu football stadium, home of Real Madrid. Inaugurated in 1947, it remains one of the world's top footballing venues. Tours are available daily (www.realmadrid.com).

Plaza de Toros, Madrid's bullfighting arena

Before his luck turned for the last time, he developed Salamanca's grid of streets as a residential refuge for the aristocracy away from the city centre. The Marqués also built Madrid's first tramways, which linked Salamanca with the centre of Madrid. The streets planned by him now have a staid, gentle and sometimes faded air, but retain smart shops and good old-fashioned restaurants.

The Marqués's own magnificent palace, long ago taken over as bank offices, stands at no. 10 on the Paseo de Recoletos. The area is crossed north to south by three major roads: Calle de Velázquez, Príncipe de Vergara and, closest to the Castellana, **Calle de Serrano**, all important shopping streets.

In its understated way, Serrano is to Madrid what Bond Street is to London or rue du Faubourg-St-Honoré to Paris: designer-label land. Here, top Spanish names such as Loewe, do business alongside foreign arrivals like Vuitton. The streets off or parallel to Serrano continue the high-end international theme. **Calle de José Ortega y Gasset** is home to Chanel (14), Dior (6) and Hermés (12), among others.

On the eastern edge of Salamanca is the **Plaza de Toros y Museo Taurino ㉖** (Bullfighting Ring and Museum; Calle de Alcalá 231; Bullfighting ring daily 10am–5.30pm, except on day of bullfights; guided tour only; museum daily 10am–5.30pm, June–Aug until 6.30pm; free; www.las-ventas.com). Officially called the Plaza de Toros Monumental de Las Ventas (and also a venue for rock concerts), this is the place to go to see a bullfight if you

◎ BULLFIGHTING

Like it or loathe it, it is hard to deny the role the *corrida* (bullfight) holds in Spanish culture. If you decide to see a bullfight, it is helpful to understand the different phases of the ritual. There are three *tercios* (acts). In the first, the bull is released, and the matador takes stock, making passes with his large pink-and-yellow *capote* (cape). The *picadores* (mounted men armed with wooden poles tipped with a *puya*, a pointed metal head) try to lance the bull behind its neck muscle, causing the bull's head to lower. In the second *tercio*, the *banderilleros* work on foot to plant long sticks, with a barbed end, into the bull's back.

The final *tercio*, the *faena*, sees the matador return, armed with just a dark red cape called a *muleta*. He adjusts his skills to the strength of the bull, with intricate passes. During the *faena*, the band will strike up an accompanying *pasodoble*; but when the matador is ready for the kill, the band stops.

It is then that the matador, *muleta* in his left hand directing the bull's attention away from his body, and sword in his right, will spin over the dangerous right horn, trying to deliver an *espada* (sword) stroke between the shoulder blades and into the heart, for an instant kill.

Madrid's bullfights at Las Ventas bullring in March, April, September and October start at 5–6pm (Sunday), while from May to August they begin at 7pm. Tickets can be purchased a day in advance, at Las Ventas (tel: 91-356 2200; 10am–2pm, 5–8pm or at www.madridbullfight.com).

can get a ticket, or simply to visit the museum of posters, capes, swords, paintings and photos. For those interested in bullfighting culture, there is also a special part dedicated to the famous matador Manolete.

GRAN VÍA, MALASAÑA AND CHUECA

The Gran Vía, a concrete canyon of American-style shopping and theatre culture, lies north of Old Madrid. It is bordered on its north side by fashionable Malasaña, Triball and Chueca, which buzz with life by day and night, and on its south side by Centro's narrow streets.

GRAN VÍA

The **Gran Vía** (Great Way) was built in three sections, begun in 1910 and completed in the early 1940s, just after the Spanish Civil War. Conceived as a grand east–west avenue, it cut a channel through the crowded, poorer quarters of the city, and was in part designed for crowd control. Until the 1960s it was Madrid's main commercial centre. Still very active, it has many hotels and high-street fashion stores.

The three stretches of the avenue are well defined. At its eastern end, nearly all the buildings have Art Nouveau details and carved stone decoration. Alfonso XIII inaugurated the construction of this section in 1910, and it was opened in

Raging bull

On 23 January 1928, a bull being led to the slaughterhouse escaped and ran amok in the Gran Vía, injuring passers-by. Diego Mazquiarán Fortuna, an elderly bullfighter living nearby, tackled the animal and killed it, an act of bravery that brought him contracts in Spain and South America.

1924. This section ends at the Red de San Luís, marked by an olive tree planted at the top of Calle de la Montera, recently pedestrianised. Once a sophisticated shopping street, it is now better known for its prostitutes, and runs down to the Puerta del Sol.

Gran Vía at night

On the opposite side of the Gran Vía, the **Edificio Telefónica** (Fuencarral 3; Tue–Sun 10am–8pm; free) augurs the start of brash commercialism. The headquarters of Telefónica, Spain's telecommunications company, was Madrid's highest building (80m/265ft) when erected in 1929. Its red clock still dominates the night skyline. Inaugurated in 2013, the **Espacio Fundación Telefónica** (https://espacio.fundaciontelefonica.com) is an art space showing changing shows with an emphasis on new technology. The panoramic views from the elevator are almost worth the visit alone.

From this point, the Gran Vía's second stretch runs to the **Plaza del Callao** – the square is named after the 1866 battle of Callao, Peru. At night, neon lights and videos flash above the cinemas' placards. This is a good spot for buying Spanish books and music at the giant Casa del Libro bookshop (No. 29; www.casadellibro.com) or at Central (Postigo de San Martín 8; www.lacentral.com), a playful book emporium with bistro, a children's zone and reading area.

The third section of the avenue, from Plaza del Callao to Plaza de España, begun in 1925, is more modern in character. Hotels, cinemas and hamburger joints predominate.

MALASAÑA

North of Callao is **Malasaña**, bordered to the east by Calle de Fuencarral and to the west by the Calle de San Bernardo. Malasaña has changed little in its grid-like layout since it was built in the 18th century. Still a rabbit warren of narrow streets, it has always had a lively street life. Nothing highlights this better than the 1808 uprising against Napoleon's troops (see page 20). In the last 10 years of Franco's rule, it was also the bohemian quarter. These days, by night it still belongs to rock 'n' roll

⊙ EL DOS DE MAYO

At the heart of Malasaña is the **Plaza Dos de Mayo** (2 May Square), formerly an artillery park connected to the 17th-century Palace of Monteleón. On 2 May 1808, during French rule, local people stormed the palace in search of weapons. As French reinforcements arrived, many locals were killed (others were later executed). The most famous victim was Manuela Malasaña, a 17-year-old embroideress who was on her way home when, according to one version of the story, she was stopped and searched by French troops who found a pair of scissors on her. The French, considering these forbidden arms, summarily executed Manuela. The two Spanish heroes of the day were Pedro Velarde and Luís Daoíz, both of whom also died. Their marble statues adorn the centre of the square under the original arched doorway of the palace. The 2nd of May is still an emotive date in Madrid, when the Plaza Dos de Mayo holds an all-day fiesta.

and the city's bar culture. By day it is home to a creative village of small shops offering alternative design, fashion, books, comics, vintage items, fun food and much more.

The heart of Malasaña is **Plaza Dos de Mayo** ㉗ (2 May Square). Both it and the surrounding streets are still populated by pensioners born in the area as well as young people attracted by its traditions. Around here, every street

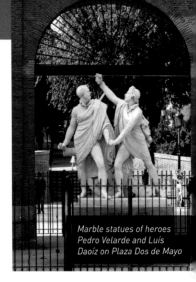

Marble statues of heroes Pedro Velarde and Luís Daoíz on Plaza Dos de Mayo

has a story. Calle Espíritu Santo (Holy Spirit Street) once bore a wooden cross in memory of a bolt of lightning that set fire to a whorehouse frequented by the disguised Felipe III. One stormy night years later, Felipe IV walked past the cross with his aides. They were set upon by thieves, and it is said that only the sword of one Don Luís de Haro saved the monarch.

One of the city's most beautiful churches is found in the middle of the quarter: the early 17th-century **San Antonio de los Alemanes** ㉘ (Mon–Sat 10.30am–2pm) in Corredera de San Pablo. Inside, the walls are covered by stunning frescoes by Giordano, Cuello and De Ricci.

Further south on Calle de Fuencarral (No. 78) stands the **Museo de Historia de Madrid** ㉙ (Tue–Sun 10am–8pm; free), built over the city's snow wells as an orphanage in the early 18th century. The splendid Baroque doorway, worth a sighting in its own right, depicts San Fernando, patron saint of orphans. Inside, in the basement, it shows a temporary collection of maps and architectural models of Madrid.

Calle de Fuencarral has become Madrid's main hip fashion zone, with dozens of local and international shoe, clothes and tattoo shops mixed in among traditional art suppliers, pharmacies and ironmongers.

To its west there are scores of bars and clubs in Malasaña. Calle San Vicente Ferrer and Calle de la Palma probably have the greatest number. The old **Juanse pharmacy** in Calle San Andres dates back to the early 1900s and has been converted into the **Juanse Kafe** specialising in Basque cooking. Colourful 19th- and early 20th-century tiled facades are a feature of the area and have been incorporated into the fronts of many modern shops and restaurants.

CHUECA

East of Calle de Fuencarral, bordered by Calle de Fernando VI, Calle Barquillo and Gran Vía, is the area of **Chueca**. After running the gamut from 19th-century affluence to 20th-century neglect, it has undergone a fashionable renaissance and is now Madrid's elegant reply to London's Soho.

Chueca's characterful narrow streets, with their mass of restaurants, bars, interior design shops, bookshops, arts and environmental businesses, run all the way to Gran Vía. Much of the business life and the buzzing street scene here is LGBTQ, and the mood is an open one which fills the *terrazas* on **Plaza de Chueca** ㉚, winter and summer alike, with Madrid's most fashionable people watchers, local and international. Clubs and music bars also abound. Its Gay Pride (Día del Orgullo) in June is one of the summer's biggest events and the quarter's own annual fiesta.

On 17 January, animals ranging from pigs to pampered poodles queue with their owners outside the **Iglesia de San Antón** (open for mass only), Calle de Hortaleza, to be blessed by the priest. Inside, the church has a fine Goya painting and St Valentine's bones. The church is the only remnant of the old leper hospital, now converted into a modern site of the Architecture Institute, restaurant, swimming pool, library, exhibition space and more.

Pooches and their owner waiting to be blessed outside Iglesia de San Antón

On the northern side of Chueca is the striking **Palacio de Longoria** ㉛ (Calle Fernando VI 6; guided tours only by appointment, tel: 91-349 9550), Madrid's only flamboyant Gaudí-style modernist building, designed as a private mansion by José Grases Riera in 1902, and today owned by the Spanish writers' and artists' copyright association (Sociedad General de Autores). Look up to the top of buildings around here and you will see fine Modernist details: lizards, penguins and other natural details. A few streets away, the **Museo Nacional de Romanticismo** ㉜ (Calle San Mateo 13; Tue–Sat 9.30am–6.30pm, May–Oct until 8.30pm, Sun and hols 10am–3pm; free Sat from 2pm and Sun; www.culturaydeporte. gob.es/mromanticismo/inicio.htm) transports you to a bourgeois city mansion in the time of Isabel II.

PLAZA DE ESPAÑA

As Gran Vía continues downhill towards the **Plaza de España**, two 1950s skyscrapers, **Torre de Madrid** and **Edificio de España**, come into sight. When you reach the centre of the square you find the **Cervantes monument** where many pay homage to the great writer: a stone sculpture honouring him looms behind bronze statues of his immortal characters, Don Quixote and Sancho Panza, astride their horse and donkey, respectively.

Calle de la Princesa, which begins at Plaza de España, is actually a northwest extension of the Gran Vía. Tucked away in extensive grounds behind high railings, the neoclassical **Palacio de Liria** at No 22 is the residence of the Duchess of Alba. The renowned family art collection includes works by Rembrandt, Titian, Rubens, Van Dyck, El Greco and Goya, but it is only open to view on Fridays. Tours are available by prior arrangement only (10am, 11am and noon; www.fundacioncasadealba.com). Nearby, on Calle Conde Duque, in the old military headquarters is the new modern cultural center with a musical and historical books library, municipal archive and the **Museo de Arte Contemporanea** (http://condeduquemadrid.es). Take a look at the **Museo ABC** (http://museo.abc.es) on Calle Maniel 29-31, dedicated to the art of drawings and illustration and located in an old brewery.

SOUTH OF PRINCESA

On Calle Ventura Rodríguez at No. 17 is the **Museo Cerralbo** ❸❸ (Tue–Sat 9.30am–3pm, also Thu 5–8pm, Sun and hols 10am–3pm; free Thu pm, Sat from 2pm, Sun; www.culturaydeporte.gob.es/mcerralbo/home.html) gives insight into the lifestyle enjoyed by the Spanish nobility during the 19th century. Don Enrique de Aguilera y Gamboa, Marqués de Cerralbo (1845–1922), was a compulsive collector, traveller and scholar. His town house, built in 1883, was bequeathed to the nation together with thousands of objets d'art. The artistic highlight is El Greco's *The Ecstasy of St Francis of Assisi* (in the chapel). No less impressive are works by Titian, Tintoretto and Alonso Cano in the Galería de Pintura and a

Templo de Debod

fine collection of Spanish *bodegones*, or still lifes. Of all the many grand rooms, the ballroom is undoubtedly the finest.

Beyond the south side of the Plaza de España is **Parque del Oeste**, a green oasis where people come to enjoy the summer and autumn sunsets. It is home to the **Templo de Debod** ❸ (closed to visitors for technical reasons until further notice). The ancient Egyptian temple was given to Spain as a gesture of thanks to the Spanish engineers involved in the Aswan Dam project.

MONCLOA AND THE WEST

At the northern end of Calle de la Princesa is **Moncloa**, home to Madrid's Complutense University. Landmarks here date from Franco's dictatorship: the air force headquarters (inspired by El Escorial) and Madrid's youngest triumphal arch, **Arco de la Victoria**, which commemorates the victory of General Franco's

Goya's frescoes in the cupola of San Antonio de la Florida

forces, when they took Madrid in 1939 after a two-year siege. Much of the area around it was destroyed during his approach.

The **Faro de Moncloa** (Avenida Arco de la Victoria, 2; Tue–Sun 9.30am–8pm) is a 100-m (330-ft) high transmission mast which was built in 1990 complete with observation deck for panoramic views. Just beyond Moncloa is the **Museo de América** ❸ (Avenida de los Reyes Católicos 6, Ciudad Universitaria; Tue–Wed and Fri–Sat 9.30am–3pm, Thu 9.30am–7pm, Sun and hols 10am–3pm; free Sun and Thu from 2pm; www.culturaydeporte.gob.es/museodeamerica/el-museo.html). Its superb collection of art and artefacts from Central and South America includes the Madrid Codex, 56 pages of bark-paper leaves, one of only four surviving examples of the Maya people's writing, and two series of the famous colonial caste paintings. You need at least two hours to enjoy the museum's entire collection which is unique in Europe.

For aficionados of Spanish art, and Goya in particular, a visit to **La Ermita de San Antonio de la Florida** ❸ (Glorieta de San Antonio de la Florida 5; Tue–Sun 9.30am–8pm; free; http://san antoniodelaflorida.es) is a must. Goya's great frescoes, remarkably preserved, covering the cupola and walls of the 18th-century chapel, mark the emergence of his free, impressionistic style after the illness which left him deaf. The narrative piece in the

cupola, capturing a street crowd, is regarded as one of his greatest achievements. The artist's tomb was installed in the church
in 1919 and in 1929 an identical chapel was built alongside this
one so Goya's frescoes and remains could rest undisturbed by
worshippers.

Next to the chapel is **Casa Mingo** (www.casamingo.es), one of
Madrid's best loved terrace restaurants, and opposite you have
access to the walking path along the city's small river, the **Río
Manzanares**, which leads back to Principe Pío station and links up
with Madrid Río, a vast landscaped riverbank area, with fountains
and bridges, running down to the Puente de Segovia. At the far
end of it, in Legazpi, is the **Matadero Madrid** (www.mataderoma-
drid.org), a modern cultural center located in an old slaughterhouse that hosts art exhibitions and has a theatre and cinema.

CASA DE CAMPO

To the west of the Río Manzanares is another former royal preserve, **Parque Casa de Campo**, forested by Felipe II in 1559. It can
be reached by car, bus, suburban railway line, metro (Lago) or
cable car (teleferico). The **cable car** (changing timetable; weekends only in winter; www.telefericomadrid.es) takes you from the
top of the Parque del Oeste across the river and into the heart
of the park, an enormous heathland of pines, shrubs, gulleys
and grassy slopes, where medieval monarchs hunted *jabalí* (wild
boar). Among the pines beneath the cable car you can see traces
of Civil War trenches from the city's three-year siege and you may
see prostitutes blatantly touting their wares on the roads that
cross the park (this is not a safe area at night).

Visitors can hire a boat on the lake, swim in open-air pools
(June–Sept), or visit the **Zoo-Aquarium** (daily from 10.30/11am,
with a changing timetable; http://zoomadrid.com), where some
150 kinds of animal pace back and forth behind moats, not bars.

There's also a funfair called the **Parque de Atracciones** (daily, with a changing timetable; http://parquedeatracciones.es).

EXCURSIONS

One of Madrid's great advantages for visitors is its position as a central leap-off point to explore Castile. El Escorial, the Valle de los Caídos, Toledo, Segovia, Aranjuez, Chinchón and Ávila are all easy day trips from the capital and you can go much further afield in a day by AVE high-speed bullet trains. If you're travelling by car, note that heavy traffic jams are typical if you head out of the city on Friday night and back into Madrid from 5pm on Sunday, particularly in summer and on holiday week-ends. A more relaxing option is to use public transport.

EL ESCORIAL

A 40-minute drive from the centre of Madrid, or a one-hour train journey, takes you to **El Real Monasterio de San Lorenzo de El Escorial** ㊲ (Tue–Sun and hols, Oct–Mar 10am–6pm, Apr–Sept 10am–8pm; free for EU citizens Wed–Thu 5–8pm in Apr–Sept and 3–6pm in Oct–Mar; www.patrimonionacional.es). El Escorial is the material realisation of the obsession of one man, Felipe II. A huge construction, built between 1563 and 1584, it takes its theme from a victory over the French in 1557 at St Quentin (now San Lorenzo's *fiesta* day), and incorporated the royal family's mausoleum. Felipe II, an introverted, deeply religious man, wanted a place in which he could retreat from his duties as king of the world's mightiest empire and be surrounded by monks, rather than courtiers, so El Escorial was designed as an austere royal residence, a library and a monastery for the Order of Hieronymites.

The enormous quadrilateral of granite stuck on to the flanks of the Sierra de Guadarrama is chillingly austere and vast: it

El Escorial

has 86 staircases and more than 2,500 windows. Its structure, with interlocking rectangles offset by spiky towers at the corners, was devised in the 16th century by Juan Bautista de Toledo and completed by Juan de Herrera.

Despite his reputation for gloomy fanaticism, Felipe II had an eye for art, and some of his best acquisitions have remained at El Escorial: canvases by Titian, Veronese and Tintoretto hang alongside works by Hieronymus Bosch and other masters from Flanders, which was then a Spanish territory. At the entrance to the Habsburg living quarters is El Greco's vast *Martyrdom of St Maurice*. Felipe II's lack of enthusiasm for this painting, now considered a masterpiece, led El Greco to settle in Toledo in search of Church patronage rather than royal commissions.

The suite of royal **living quarters** reflects Felipe's austere personal habits and piety. Everything is sparse in the study from which he ruled an empire and the attached bedroom has views of the basilica's altar.

In contrast, the richly decorated **Royal Pantheon**, located under the altar of the vast basilica, holds the remains of 23 kings and queens of Spain – the latter being admitted only if they had become the mother of a future sovereign. Felipe V, who loathed El Escorial, and Fernando VI are absent, by their own request. The last royal figure to be laid to rest here was Juan de Borbón, who was obliged by General Franco to cede his rights to the throne in favour of his son, Spain's present King Juan Carlos I. Juan de Borbón died in Pamplona on 1 April 1993 and was interred two days later, earning his place as the son and father of kings, though he was never a king himself.

El Escorial's spectacular gilded library

El Escorial's **library** is said to rank second only to the Vatican's in quality. The gilt edges of the books face outwards on the shelves to preserve the spines. Pope Gregory XII ordered the excommunication of anyone who stole a manuscript from here.

The town's tourist office (www.sanlorenzoturismo.org) is adjacent to the palace. Ask for a free map to find your way to the **Casita del Príncipe** (Casita de Abajo), set in a park below the palace, and to the **Casita del Infante** (Casita de Arriba), a shorter but more strenuous stroll uphill, following the Paseo de Carlos III. (Both may be visited during the same hours as the main palace for an extra charge.) These late 18th-century pleasure palaces were built for the sons of Carlos III and are furnished as opulently as any of Madrid's fully-fledged royal residences.

VALLE DE LOS CAÍDOS

Just around the mountain is another monument of enormous proportions, but far more polemical. After the Spanish Civil War, Franco wanted to build a monument to commemorate those who died during the hostilities. For the site he chose the V-shaped valley called Cuelgamuros known today as the **Valle de los Caídos** (Valley of the Fallen). The most visible part of the monument is a huge cross standing 150m (492ft) high, set upon the summit of a small mountain. Equally grand is the underground **Basilica** open to the public (Tue–Sun 10am–7pm, until 6pm Oct–Mar; www.valledeloscaidos. es). Carved 240m (786ft) deep into the granite mountain, using prisoner-of-war labour from the Republican forces, the basilica is reached via a tunnel. The tombs of Franco and José Antonio Primo de Rivera, founder of the Falangist Party, occupy a privileged position, making this a place of homage for his followers. Ossuaries in the crypt (closed to the public) contain the remains of tens of thousands of the dead, of both

Valle de los Caídos monument

sides, from the Civil War, making private reburial impossible, despite descendants' requests.

TOLEDO

If you have just one day available for an excursion from Madrid, **Toledo** 🔞, the country's Visigothic capital in the 6th century, is a good choice. Originally a Roman fortress, it reached its zenith in the Muslim period and after the Christian Reconquest by Alfonso VI in the 11th century, when it became capital of Castile. Alfonso was crowned emperor of Spain and a two-century 'Golden Age' ensued. The court's transfer to Madrid in 1561 triggered the economic decline of the former capital.

To enjoy Toledo's history and beauty at its best you need to work around the massive influx of tourists it receives on day excursions. Even Toledo's renowned steel craftsmen, whose traditional skills such as 'damascening' – cutting pigmented patterns in the metal – are rooted in the city's Moorish heritage, have had to take action against the producers of thousands of trashy items sold as souvenirs. The best way to avoid the crowds and enjoy the historic centre is to stay overnight (https://turismo.toledo.es).

A good place to start a visit is **Museo de Los Concilios y Cultura Visigoda** Ⓐ (Iglesia de San Roman; Tue–Sat 10am–2pm and 4–6pm, Sun 9am–3pm), which explores the city's Visigothic legacy. It is housed in the beautiful 13th-century *mudéjar* church of **San Roman**, which was probably built on the ruins of an earlier mosque, which in turn was built on the site of a Visigoth church. Such are the layers of Toledo's history.

Before the structure of the Church crystallised and Toledo's cathedral became the symbol of its power, there was a period of relative tolerance in the late Middle Ages when Islam, Christianity and Judaism coexisted quite comfortably. Their famed *convivencia*, as it is known, produced a cultural flowering expressed in medicine and the sciences, literature and translation, architecture and the arts. In particular, the *mudéjar* architecture and decoration created by Muslim craftsmen who stayed in Spain after the Reconquest reached a high point here between the 12th and 16th centuries. It was adopted by the Jewish community, too, after the onset of Christian persecution in the 14th century.

Two historic synagogues stand on the southwestern slope of the city – the **Sinagoga del Tránsito** ⓑ (Tue–Sat Nov–Feb 9.30am–6pm, Mar–Oct until 7.30pm, Sun 10am–3pm), built for Pedro the Cruel's treasurer, Samuel Levi, in the second half of the 14th century and today containing the small Museo Sefardí; and the 13th-century **Sinagoga de Santa María la Blanca** ⓒ (daily 10am–5.45pm, summer until 6.45pm). Both show strong Moorish influence in their design, with horseshoe arches, arabesques and glazed tiles. By contrast, all that remains of the Muslim past is the **Mezquita Cristo de la Luz** ⓓ, later converted into a church, above the Puerta del Sol; and the **Puerta de la Bisagra**, the main entry point for visitors coming from Madrid.

The **Catedral** ⓔ (Mon–Sat 10am–6pm, Sun 2–6pm; www.catedralprimada.es) is one of Spain's most spectacular sights. It is visible from any part of town thanks to its Gothic tower topped by a spire ringed by spikes. Built between the 13th and 15th centuries, it is remarkable for its design, the carvings and paintings in its chapels and choir

Toledo

Toledo at sunset

and later accumulated additions. It remains the first seat of the Primate of Spain. The Sacristy contains works by El Greco, Goya, Van Dyke and Bellini. Other highlights include the frescoed chapter house and the 16th-century stained glass in the transept.

El Greco's masterpiece, *The Burial of the Count of Orgaz*, is on display in the **Iglesia de Santo Tomé** **F**, close to the cathedral (daily 10am–5.45pm, Mar–Oct until 6.45pm; www. santotome.org). The artist painted himself into the picture – he's the seventh figure from the left at the bottom, staring straight ahead. Earlier paintings in the **Convento de Santo Domingo de Silos** **G**, where he and his wife were buried, are also of interest. In this area, too, stands the **Museo del Greco** **H** (Paseo del Transito; Tue–Sat 9.30am–7.30pm, Nov–Feb until 6pm; Sun and hols 10am–3pm; free Sat from 4pm and Sun; www.culturaydeporte.gob.es/mgreco/inicio.

Toledo's Catedral and Alcázar

html), refurbished for the 400th anniversary of El Greco's death in 2014, with the recreation of the old painter's house and modern exhibition spaces.

Near the **Plaza de Zocodover**, in the heart of Toledo, is the **Museo de Santa Cruz** ❶ (Mon–Sat 10am–6pm, Sun 9am–3pm; Wed pm), a fine Renaissance building displaying more works by El Greco, Ribera and Goya.

Beyond the city walls, in the northern district of Las Covachuela, the **Hospital de Tavera** ❶ (daily 10am–1.30pm and 3–5.30pm) exhibits works by El Greco, Tintoretto, Titian, Zurbarán and Ribera.

Dominating the city is the enormous **Alcázar** ❶ (Tue–Sun 10am–5pm; free on Sun; www.museo.ejercito.es), a fortress destroyed and rebuilt many times since the Roman era. The fortress now houses a five-storey **Army Museum** with displays relating to the dramatic 72-day siege.

Travelling to Toledo by train will enable you to admire its grand neo-*mudéjar* **railway station**, built for Alfonso XIII's visits to the city. In the 1920s, this was the starting point for evenings of the Grand Order of Toledo, a group of surrealists, including Salvador Dalí and Luis Buñuel, who met with the sole object of drinking the night away in good company in Toledo.

If you're driving back to Madrid from Toledo and want to make a brief stop, the village of **Illescas** (33km/20 miles from Toledo) keeps five paintings by El Greco, which hang in the church of the local Hospital de la Virgen de la Caridad (Convent of the Virgin of Charity; www.elgrecoillescas.com).

SEGOVIA

Located 88km (55 miles) northwest of Madrid, now easily reached by AVE high-speed train (45 minutes and frequent buses or taxis), **Segovia** ㊴ rises majestically from the surrounding plains. The city's setting is picturesque *campo* – wide-open

---

⦿ EL GRECO IN TOLEDO

El Greco spent the most productive years of his prolific career in Toledo. Just down the hill from Santo Tomé, the El Greco house – misleadingly named, since the artist almost certainly never lived in it – has been reconstructed and linked to a museum dedicated to his life. Still, it has authentic 16th-century furnishings and a tranquil garden that replicate the look and feel of a Toledan house of the era. Several of the master's paintings are on display, among them *A View of Toledo* and *Portrait of St Peter*. The El Greco house was originally built by Samuel Levi, a 14th-century Jewish financier and friend of King Pedro the Cruel of Castile.

plains interrupted by an occasional monastery or castle – with the slopes of the Sierra de Guadarrama filling half the horizon.

Segovia is a city of great monuments, all testament to epochs of glory: a 2,000-year-old aqueduct, a fine cathedral and a later storybook *alcázar*. It also has dozens of smaller churches, cultural sites and experiences that may be visited seasonally (www.turismodesegovia.com)

The wondrous **Roman Aqueduct Ⓐ**, a work of art and a triumph of engineering, marches right across the entrance of the town. The aqueduct is composed of thousands of granite blocks arranged in graceful arches, sometimes two-tiered, but without mortar or cement. It is nearly 1km (0.5 miles) long, and it rises to a height of 46m (150ft). This is the last lap of a conduit that brought water from a mountain stream to the walled city. The aqueduct was in constant use for 100 generations, with only a couple of details changed. In the 16th century, a statue of Hercules in a niche over the tallest arch was replaced by a Christian image.

The **Alcázar Ⓑ**, Segovia's fairytale royal castle (daily Apr–Oct 10am–8pm, Nov–Mar until 6pm; free Tue 2–4pm only EU citizens; www.alcazardesegovia.com), was erected on a ridge overlooking the confluence of two rivers, with an unimpeded view of the plateau in all directions. The Romans are thought to have built a watchtower here. The present castle, reportedly the model for the first Disneyland, is a far cry from the simple stone fortress that took shape in the 12th century. As the fortress grew bigger and more luxurious, it also came to play a significant historical role. By the 13th century, parliaments were convened here. The most fanciful and photogenic parts of the castle's superstructure – its feast of turrets and towers – are the work of restoration after a disastrous fire in 1862. A hefty climb up the tower will be rewarded by breathtaking views of Segovia and the valley beyond.

From whatever part of town you view it, the **Catedral** 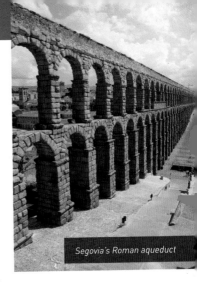 (Nov–Mar 9.30am–6.30pm, Apr–Oct 9am–9.30pm, tower daily guided tours Oct–Mar at 10.30am, 12.30pm, 4.30pm, Apr–Sept at 7pm; http://catedralsegovia.es) is a beautiful sight. Its pinnacles, buttresses and cupolas seem to belong to a whole complex of churches. Begun in 1525 (but not consecrated until 1768), this is the last of the great Spanish Gothic cathedrals.

Segovia's Roman aqueduct

Inside, the cathedral's majestic columns and arches are lit by fine stained-glass windows. Two 18th-century organs are spectacularly flamboyant. Less obvious are the altarpieces in the chapels, the most important element of which is a 16th-century polychrome *Pietŕ* by the Valencian Juan de Juan, just to the right of the entrance.

Delicate arches line the cloister, which belonged to a former cathedral that was destroyed and was moved here, stone by stone, in the 16th century. The adjacent museum and chapter house contain a number of interesting pieces of religious art and relics, including 17th-century tapestries, the Baroque carriage propelled through the streets of Segovia every Corpus Christi (in June), and the reminder of a 14th-century tragedy: the tomb of the infant Prince Pedro, son of Enrique II. He slipped from the arms of his nurse as she admired the view from an open window of the

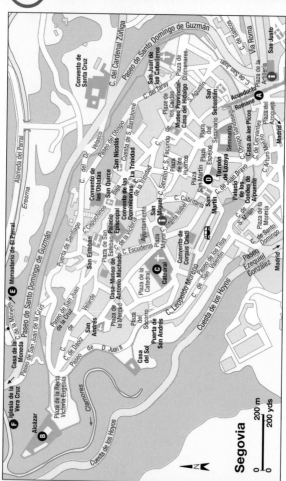

Segovia

0 ____ 200 m
0 ____ 200 yds

Alcázar. Legend has it she scarcely hesitated before she leaped after him to her death in the moat below.

Segovia's main square, the **Plaza Mayor**, combines history with real-life bustle. The 17th-century town hall faces the large oblong plaza where shoppers, businessmen and tourists take time out for coffee in the fresh air.

A few streets away to the east, a church much older than the cathedral

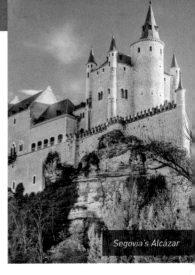
Segovia's Alcázar

graces Segovia's loveliest square. La Iglesia de San Martín is a 12th-century Romanesque beauty with glorious portals and porches (open for mass only). **Plaza de San Martín** **D**, which slopes down to Calle de Juan Bravo, is surrounded by noble mansions. Next to the church, the building with stark, barred windows was built as a prison in the 17th century; it now houses a library. Here and throughout the city, the facades of buildings are subject to elaborate three-dimensional decoration, mainly with geometric forms. The most unusual example, the nearby Casa de los Picos, bristles with pointed protuberances.

Total tranquillity permeates the **Monasterio de El Parral** **E** (Wed–Sat guided visits at 11am and 5pm; donation), founded in the mid-15th century just beyond the city walls but within easy reach of the centre of town. The architectural details, including a Gothic cloister, are being restored in fits and starts.

Segovia's skyline

After a Sunday morning visit, you can hear a sung Mass, with Gregorian chant.

Also just outside the wall and almost in the shadow of the Alcázar, is the stunning **Iglesia de la Vera Cruz** Ⓕ (Wed–Sun 10.30am–1.30pm and 4–6pm, Tue only pm), a 12-sided structure dating from the early 13th century. The knights of the Holy Sepulchre held court in its unique double-decker chapel, surrounded by a circular nave.

ARANJUEZ

A 40-minute journey south of Madrid by train or bus lies **Aranjuez** ㊵ (www.aranjuez.es), its setting beside the River Tagus highlighted by its splendid Royal Palace. The **Real Palacio de Aranjuez** (Tue–Sun 10am–6pm, Apr–Sept until 8pm; free for EU citizens Wed–Thu 5–8pm in Apr–Sept and 3–6pm in Oct–Mar; www.patrimonionacional.es) was built by Felipe II and rebuilt during the reign of Fernando VI after a fire in 1748 destroyed most of the interior but left the original 16th-century structure intact. Carlos IV and his queen, María Luisa, furnished it to the hilt. Here you will see a porcelain-lined room even more elaborate than the one in Madrid's Royal Palace. Goya's portrait of Fernando VII shows him for the brutish dictator he turned out to be. The chandeliers are particularly fine. One of the studies is filled with 203 framed watercolour sketches that make for an illustrated encyclopaedia of life in China during the mid-19th century, with customs, trades, temples, flora and fauna meticulously depicted. These were a gift from the Emperor of China to Isabel II. During her reign, too, the smoking room was decorated in layers of stucco to reproduce the Tower of the Two Sisters at the Alhambra, with the red, green and gold colours that have faded from the original.

But in many respects, the Palace of Aranjuez is outdone by its satellite, the **Casita del Labrador** (Worker's Cottage), a rococo-style pavilion built for Carlos IV in response to the Petit Trianon at Versailles. Situated at the far end of the royal gardens, it is packed with 18th-century bric-à-brac.

Aranjuez is equally visited for its parks and gardens. The most beautiful are the 18th-century Jardín de la Isla and Jardín del Principe (Garden Island and Prince's Garden; daily from 8am, closing times vary; free).

CHINCHÓN

The picture-postcard town of **Chinchón** ④, 52km (32

Strawberry train

On summer weekends you can travel from Madrid to Aranjuez by a special train, the Tren de las Fresas, on which strawberries (fresas) are handed out by girls wearing traditional costumes. Tickets cost about €30 (www.museodelferrocarril.org).

miles) south of Madrid and a 10-minute bus or car ride east of Aranjuez, remains surprisingly rural. It is famous for its historic **Plaza Mayor**, used for bullfights since at least 1502 and as the setting for a renowned Passion Play on the evening of Easter Saturday. Surrounded by three-storey wooden galleries, the *plaza* is both rustic and elegant.

Chinchón (www.ciudadchinchon.com) is famous for its bars in which you can try the local aniseed-based tipple, *anís*, and restaurants serving charcoal-grilled *chorizo* and meat, which may be cooked with the excellent local garlic, another speciality.

ÁVILA

From Madrid, road and rail routes climb through spectacular woodlands, streams and rugged peaks to reach Ávila province, a wild tundra-like plateau dotted with wind-eroded shrubs and huge boulders. This austere landscape – a source of inspiration for St Teresa and other saints – is one of the highest inhabited areas in Spain.

Its provincial capital, located approximately 100km (60 miles) northwest of Madrid, is the medieval walled city of **Ávila** ⓬ (www.avilaturismo.com). Ávila is the highest provincial capital in Spain so until as late as April it can be bitterly cold up there. The **Muralla**, or city wall – over 2km (1.2 miles) long and with no

Musical inspiration

The most popular guitar concerto ever, Joaquín Rodrigo's Concierto de Aranjuez was inspired by the beautiful river gardens at the Palacio Real. The music transports the listener to the palace surrounded by nature; Rodrigo described it as 'capturing the fragrance of magnolias, the singing of birds and the gushing of fountains'.

less than 88 watchtowers and nine gates – is the best preserved in Europe. It may be climbed via two points of access, El Alcázar and Casa de Las Carnicerías (Tue–Sun late Oct–late Mar 10am–6pm, late Mar–June and Sept–late Oct until 8pm, July–Aug until 9pm; http://muralladeavila.com), now the tourist office. The apse of the **Catedral** (July–Aug Mon–Sat 10am–9pm, Sun 11.45am–9pm, Sept–Oct

The medieval walls of Ávila

and Apr–June Mon–Fri 10am–8pm, Sat until 9pm, Sun and hols 11.45am–7.30pm, Nov–Mar Mon–Fri 10am–6pm, Sat until 7pm, Sun and hols 11.45am–5.30pm; http://catedralavila.es) sticks out to form a part of these fortifications. The city has been a magnet for pilgrims ever since the late 16th century, as the birthplace of St Teresa, the great reformer of the Carmelite Order. Visitors can see Teresa's birthplace, now marked by a 17th-century church; the convent where she lived much of her life, the Monasterio de Encarnación; and the Convento de San José, the first she founded in the city.

Other notable sights include the **Basílica de San Vicente**, built on the site where San Vicente and his two sisters were martyred in the 4th century; and the 15th-century Monasterio de Santo Tomé, with its three haunting cloisters and marble tomb of Fernando and Isabel's only son, Don Juan, who died aged 19.

Flamenco performance

WHAT TO DO

SHOPPING

Madrid's major department stores are located in the centre between the Puerta del Sol and Callao, and along the Gran Vía. More select designers line Calle de Serrano and its adjoining streets in Salamanca. Calle del Prado, La Latina and Puerta de Toledo are good for antiques. For high-street shops try Calle del Arenal, Sol, Calle de Preciados, Gran Vía and Calle de la Princesa. Calle de Fuencarral is the city's main drag for hip young fashion from home and abroad, with more expensive one-off designs in Chueca in newer alternative shops scattered through Malasaña and its subzone Triball.

Madrid's major department-store chain is El Corte Inglés (branches at Calle de Serrano 47; Calle de Preciados 3; Calle de la Princesa 41; Calle de Goya 76, on the corner of Calle del Alcalá; and Calle Raimundo Fernández Villaverde 1). Note that department stores often offer a 10 percent discount to foreign shoppers (ask in the store for details).

Among Madrid's central shopping centres **La Vaguada** (Avenida Monforte de Lemos s/n, Barrio del Pilar; www.enla vaguada.com), in northern Madrid, is a multi-level complex with 300 shops, bars, restaurants and cinemas. **ABC Serrano** (Calle de Serrano 61; http://abcserrano.com) is the most central mall, but smaller, with selected stylish shops, café and restaurant.

Only shopping centres and department stores are guaranteed to stay open through the day. Opening hours are generally Monday–Friday, 9 or 10am until 1.30pm or 2pm, and 4pm or 5pm until 8pm. On Saturday, stores tend to open from 9.30am until 1.30pm. Sunday opening has taken off in the city centre, particularly around Puerta del Sol and Gran Via, but is not yet general through the city.

WHAT TO BUY

There's no shortage of items to take home, from traditional Spanish fans to foodstuffs or cutting-edge fashions.

Books: There's an outdoor second-hand book stand open daily on Pasadizo de San Ginés, off Calle del Arenal, and on Cuesta de Moyano, near Atocha, at weekends. From late May, a book fair takes over the Retiro for several weeks. Antonio Machado (Marqués de Casa Riera 2 and Fernando VI 17; www.machado-libros.com) is a good Spanish bookshop. La Central de Callao,

⊙ THE RASTRO

On Sunday morning Madrid's most famous street market, the Rastro, selling everything from antiques, books and fashions to pets and coal-burning stoves, spreads through Lavapiés from Tirso de Molina to Ronda de Embajadores. A good starting point for exploring the quarter is the Plaza del Cascorro, while further down the Ribera de Curtidores – the market's main avenue – is the rastro itself, the slaughterhouse after which the market is named.

Some of the most interesting finds are on and around the Plaza General Vara del Rey, where antiques stalls and shops sell second-hand cameras, books and postcards. If you seriously want to buy, arrive by 9.30am. By midday the streets are packed. Be on the alert for pickpockets – this is unfortunately a notorious place for thieving.

Leave time for some tapas in one of the busy bars. The Rastro starts to pack up about 3pm.

Postigo de San Martín 8, open daily 10am–9.30pm, stocks gifts, cards and magazines as well as a huge array of carefully stocked books.

Crafts: The streets below Plaza Mayor have unusual craft shops. Casa Hernanz (Calle Toledo 18; www. casahernanz.es), specialises in espadrilles (*alpargatas*), Cerería Ortega (Calle Toledo 43; www.cereriaortega.es) in candles and the Corchera Castellana (Cava Baja 47) in cork items.

Fans for keeping cool

Antiques: Head to the Rastro. In nearby streets are more solid establishments dealing in old objets d'art.

Fashion: Spanish fashion has produced major brands and designers in the last three decades. For the big couture names, head for Salamanca – on Calle de Serrano, look for Hoss Intropia (No. 18; www.intropia.com), Loewe (No. 34; www.loewe.com). For high street and budget fashion, explore Calle de Fuencarral. Zara – the largest branch, with two shop spaces, is at Gran Vía 52–54. Custo and Camper (Fuencarral 29 and 42) are key brands.

Flamenco: Music, clothes and instruments are found at El Flamenco Vive (Conde de Lemos 7; www.elflamencovive.com), close to Opera.

Food and Drink: Lavinia (Calle José Ortega y Gasset 16; www. lavinia.es) stocks over 2,000 Spanish wines, including Sherry (*jerez*), and Rioja and Ribera del Duero red and white *crianzas*, *door bookshop on Pasadizo de San Ginés*

reservas and *gran reservas*. The municipal markets are an unmissable experience for food lovers (Anton Martín in Lavapiés and La Paz in Salamanca are good examples). The gourmet food departments of El Corte Inglés have a good range too.

Leather: Salvador Bachiller (Gran Vía 65 and other branches; www.salvadorbachiller.com) makes stunning bags, suitcases, wallets and other items in a huge range of colours.

ENTERTAINMENT

NIGHTLIFE

Madrid nightlife is hectic, fast-moving and carries on all night. In the early 1980s, *la movida*, the arts and nightlife nurtured by the socialist mayor, Enrique Tierno Galván, created such a sense of street fiesta that exhausted people would sigh, *Madrid me mata*

– Madrid is killing me. Constantly in search of the ultimate in *marcha*, or fun, young Madrileños flock into the city centre after work, usually from Thursday to Saturday and at least until sunrise.

Good starting points for an evening stroll are the *cervecerías* on the Plaza Santa Ana (sedate), the central boulevard of the Paseo del Prado (smart), or the *tascas* and *tavernas* in Huertas (young), where you can have a bite to eat before things get going in the clubs, bars and discos. In Malasaña, Plaza Dos de Mayo is peppered with alternative bars; while Chueca, to the north of the Gran Vía, the vibrant centre of Madrid's LGBTQ scene, is the hip equivalent of New York's SoHo, with dozens of gay and hetero bars, clubs and restaurants.

Madrid nightlife provides a wealth of cultural experiences. Our top choices are listed below:

Live music clubs. There are plenty of places in Madrid for live jazz and Latin music. **Café Central** (Plaza del Ángel 10; www.cafecentralmadrid.com) is a long-standing jazz café near Plaza de Santa Ana, with nightly music. **Populart** (Calle de las Huertas 22; http://cafepopulart.com) has a more wide-ranging line-up including jazz, reggae and blues. **Clamores** (Albuquerque 14; www.salaclamores.es) also has interesting programming.

After-hours clubs. Venues, the sessions they host and prices change all the time. Here's a sample of some highlights between Wednesday and Sunday nights: **Monnalisa Madrid**, Calle de Núñez de Arce 8, hip-hop, rock (Tue–Sun 10pm–3/3.30am); **Changó**, in Covarrubias 42, electronic (Fri–Sat 8pm–5am); **Teatro Kapital**, Calle Atocha 125

What's on

To find out what is on, consult the magazine *Guía del Ocio* (www.guiadelocio.com), out every Friday and available from kiosks.

(Thu–Sat from midnight till 5.30/6am), seven independent floors pump any kind of music till dawn; **El Sol** on Calle Jardines 3, a legendary movida's venue offers indie, rock and alternative music (Tue–Sat 10pm–5.30am, current entry cost €12).

MUSIC AND THEATRE

Classical music, opera and dance. As home to the National Orchestra, the Spanish Radio and Television Symphony, the Compania Nacional de Danza (contemporary), the Ballet Nacional de España, and the city's and region's orchestras and dance companies, Madrid has an exceptional calendar of concerts, recitals and dance events.

⊙ FLAMENCO

Spain's most unique art form is flamenco, built around its song, guitars, and – perhaps best known – its dance with percussive heels. Pure flamenco, which has grown around *cante jondo* (deep song) deals with human dramas of poverty, love and death in a slow, piercing manner. You can watch flamenco in clubs across the capital, including: **Café de Chinitas** (Calle Torija 7; www.chinitas.com; Metro: Santo Domingo); **Corral de la Morería** (Calle de la Morería 17; www.corraldelamoreria.com; Metro: Opera); **Casa Patas** (Calle Cañizares 10; www.casapatas.com; Metro: Antón Martín), a restaurant-bar with flamenco shows in a back room (shows at 8 and 10.30pm) and **Las Tablas** (Plaza de España 9; www.lastablasmadrid.com) which offers a more modern setting than traditional flamenco shows. However, many of the best performances are given in theatres and concert halls – check the newspaper for dates.

Madrid's opera house, the **Teatro Real**, features big-name productions (Plaza Isabel II; www.teatro-real.com).

The **Auditorio Nacional de Música** (Príncipe de Vergara 146; www.auditorionacional.mcu.es) has excellent seasons of recitals and concerts, including experimental contemporary music and flamenco, throughout the year.

Madrileños enjoying a concert

The **Teatro de la Zarzuela** (Calle de Jovellanos 4; http://teatrodelazarzuela.mcu.es) and **Teatros del Canal** (Calle Cea Bermúdez 1; www.teatroscanal.com) are Madrid's main contemporary, classical and world dance venues.

Theatre. Spain's dramatic tradition is long and glorious. In dozens of Madrid theatres, classical and contemporary foreign and Spanish works are performed. Among those with the greatest critical acclaim are the following: **Teatro de Abádia** (Calle Fernández de los Ríos 42; www.teatroabadia.com), at the former Church of La Sagrada Familia, offers quality contemporary drama. **Teatro de la Comedia** (Calle del Príncipe 14) puts on classic Spanish works, by playwrights such as Federico García Lorca and Lope de Vega. **Teatro Español** (Calle del Príncipe 25; www.teatroespanol.es) and its new warehouse space, the **Matadero**, set the pace for excellent classic and contemporary international and home-grown theatre.

Estadio Santiago Bernabéu

Cinema. Details of subtitled films shown in their original language (*version original* or VO) are published in the weekly Guía del Ocio and in daily papers such as *El País* and in *El Mundo's* Friday magazine *Metropoli* (www.elmundo.es/metropoli.html). The main cluster of VO cinemas, totalling 18 screens in all, is on Martín de los Heros and Princesa (Cines Yelmo, Princesa, Renoir Plaza de España and Renar Princesa).

Teletickets. Most theatre, dance, opera and some cinema tickets can be bought on the web. Try www.entradas.com or www.elcorteingles.es.

SPORTS

Basketball. Games are held in the Real Madrid Baloncesto installations, north of the Plaza de Castilla, or in the Palacio de Deportes on Avenida Felipe II. Two teams at the top of the Spanish league are Adecco Estudiantes and Real Madrid.

Fútbol (football/soccer). The world's number one sport is a passion in Spain. The two big Madrid teams are **Real Madrid** and **Atlético Madrid**. Tickets for Real Madrid matches can be obtained daily 6–9pm from their central stadium: Estadio Santiago Bernabéu, Avenida de Concha Espina, by Tower A

(Metro: Santiago Bernabéu; tel: 902-324 324; www.realmadrid. es). Tickets for Atlético Madrid can be obtained daily 11am– 2pm and 5–8pm, as well as on match days from 11am to kick-off at their stadium in the southerly area of Piramides beside the River Manzanares: Estadio Vicente Calderón, Po Virgen del Puerto 67 (Metro: Piramides); tel: 902-260 403.

Golf. There are 22 golf courses in the Madrid area. Greens are open to non-members on payment of a substantial greens fee. Contact the Real Federación Española de Golf, Capitán Haya 9, 28020 Madrid; www.rfegolf.es.

Skiing. From December to April, the Guadarrama mountains north of Madrid become a ski area. The scenery and facilities are first-rate, and all equipment may be hired. The most highly developed resort, with five ski-chairs and six ski-lifts, is Navacerrada (www.puertonavacerrada.com), only 52km (32 miles) from Madrid, along the N6012. Expect the slopes to be packed when there is snow. **Valdesquí**, reached via the N1 and N601, 150km (92 miles) from Madrid, has six ski-lifts, a ski-school and a ski-tow. For more details, see www.infonieve.es.

Elsewhere in Madrid, various sports facilities cater to many interests. You'll find tennis courts, polo grounds, squash courts, swimming pools and riding stables.

CHILDREN'S MADRID

The **Casa de Campo**, with its teleférico (cable car), funfair (Parque de Atracciones, see page 70), lake and open-air swimming is a good option on hot days. Also within the Casa de Campo, there's the **Madrid ZooAquarium**. The year-round circus at Circo Price (Rda de Toledo 35; www.teatrocircoprice. es) is a reliable choice too.

Attractions in the **Parque del Buen Retiro** include marionette shows at noon on Sundays and rowing on the lake (see page 52).

At **Safari Madrid** (Aldea del Fresno, National Highway V, near Navalcarnero; daily 10.30am–5.30pm; www.safarimadrid. com), elephants, rhinos, lions and zebra roam freely, and you can also get close up to birds of prey, insects and reptiles.

Closer to the city is **Faunia** (Avenida de la Comunidades 28, Metro: Valdebernardo; www.faunia.es), a hugely successful theme park simulating a variety of ecosystems and their fauna.

Aquopolis (Avenida de la Dehesa, Villanueva de la Cañada; mid-June–Sept; tel: 91-815 6911; https://villanueva.aquopolis. es) is a large waterpark with wave pools, shoots, cascades and toddlers' pools. Free buses go from the city centre; check the website for details.

Another attraction is the **Planetario de Madrid** (Planetarium; Parque Tierno Galván; Metro: Méndez Álvaro; tel: 91-467 3461; www.planetmad.es), where shows start at 5.30pm and 6.30pm Tue–Fri and 11am, noon, 1pm, 5.30pm and 6.30pm at weekends and holidays. **Imaginarium** (Puerto de la Habana 26 and other branches) is an exceptionally creative toyshop (www. imaginarium.es). The National Museum of Natural Sciences (Calle José Gutierrez Abascal 2; Tue–Fri 10am–5pm, Sat–Sun until 8pm; www.mncn.csic.es), with thousands of minerals, algae, plants, animals of all kinds, stones, tools and arms from various cultures and ages, will keep children busy for hours.

Located halfway between Madrid and Aranjuez, at San Martín de la Vega, **Parque Warner Madrid** (Ctra M301 km 15.5, tel: 912-000 792; www.parquewarner.com) offers five themed areas incorporating sets and characters from Warner Brothers films and cartoons. Among the attractions is an 80kmh (50mph) roller-coaster.

CALENDAR OF EVENTS

As you plan your excursions, it is worth checking additional details of festivals and fairs with tourist information offices.

January *Día de los Reyes* (Three Kings Cavalcade). Procession commemorating the kings' pilgrimage to meet baby Jesus. *San Anton*. Blessing of pets and animals at San Anton church, Calle Haraleza.

February *Carnaval*. Week before Lent celebrated with the Entierro de la Sardina (Burial of the Sardine) on Paseo de la Florida. ARCO (Contemporary Art Fair), Spain's largest international art fair.

March/April Semana Santa (Holy Week). Every town and city has striking processions. In cities with famous cathedrals, such as Toledo and Segovia, the spectacle is unforgettable.

May *Madrid: Fiestas de San Isidro* (St Isidore the Husbandman), the capital's patron saint. Half a month of neighbourhood parties, plays, concerts and daily bullfights.

June **Toledo**: *Corpus Christi*. The Spanish primate leads a solemn religious procession through the medieval streets. *Toledo Province: Camuñas*. An ancient religious play is presented in mime, with spectacular costumes. *Fiestas de San Juan and San Pedro*. Dances, bullfights, fireworks.

July *Ávila*. Outdoor festival with poetry, art, theatre, sports and bullfights.

July–August *Madrid: Veranos* de la Villa. Open-air festival of music and dance in central Madrid venues.

August *Madrid: Castizo* fiestas, the traditional fiestas of San Caeyetano, San Lorenzo and La Virgen de la Paloma, with much of the activity taking place around the Plaza de la Paja and the Jardines de las Vistillas. 15 August is a major national holiday and many towns have local celebrations.

October–November *Festival de Otoño*. The city's biggest cultural festival includes international theatre, jazz, dance and other events.

December *Nochevieja* (New Year's Eve). Celebration in Puerta del Sol; grapes are swallowed between each chime of the clock.

EATING OUT

Madrid is a food lover's city: its restaurants are for those with every kind of budget and you can sample Spain's regional cuisine from around the country and world cuisine from Latin America to Asia. Apart from this, you cannot miss the city's take on the *tapeo*, the tapas crawl. Regional cuisine varies greatly, but Spanish cooking is never overly spicy; however, it is garlicky and liberally salted.

MEALTIMES

For many visitors, eating hours in Spain take some getting used to. *Madrileños* eat lunch and dinner late by most

Selection of tapas

standards. Lunch usually isn't begun until 2 or 3pm and friends often meet for dinner at 9.30–10pm. Outside local hours you are likely to find yourself dining alone. Swing into local habits and pace yourself, Spanish style, by grazing on tapas at your normal dinner time.

RESTAURANTS AND MENUS

Spaniards traditionally eat three courses at both lunch and dinner. However, it's not uncommon to share a first course, or to order *un sólo plato* (just a main course), if you're not that hungry. Many restaurants offer bargain lunchtime set menus called the *menú del día*. For a fixed price (usually €8–15 in an everyday eatery, and €25–40 in a gourmet restaurant), you'll get a choice of first course, a main dish and dessert or coffee, plus a glass of either wine (or more), beer or bottled water, and bread.

Restaurants feature a grading system, from five forks to one, marked on the door of the restaurant. The system is an indication of price, and grades the facilities and service, not the quality of the food.

While restaurants offer a full menu, often with a fixed-price menu available, cafeterías usually focus on *platos combinados*, which combine main courses and accompaniments such as steak, eggs, chips and salad served on the same plate.

Most bars and *cervecerías* (draft beer bars) also serve tapas, sandwiches (*bocadillos*) or limited *platos combinados*. In summer their pavement terraces will look alluring, but remember, prices are higher if you sit at a table or outside rather than at the bar.

The most insignificant meal of the day in Spain is generally breakfast, except at hotels, which offer continental breakfasts or buffets. A true Madrid breakfast is *churros*, fritters, sometimes

Chocolate con churros

made before your eyes. You can dunk *churros* in your coffee, or eat them as Spaniards do, with extremely thick, strong hot chocolate.

CASTILIAN SPECIALITIES

Cocido madrileño is one of many regional variations of the originally medieval, possibly Jewish one-pot stew found all over Spain. The meal often starts with *sopa de cocido*, the broth resulting from boiling the ingredients for the next course, before moving to the *cocido* itself: beef, cured ham, sausage, chickpeas, cabbage, onion and potatoes.

Another speciality is Castilian soup, also known as *sopa de ajo* or garlic soup. At the last moment, a raw egg is added to the soup, and by the time it reaches the table, the egg is well poached.

Callos a la madrileña is stewed tripe – try it if you like spicy-hot tomato sauce. For a lighter speciality, try *besugo al horno*, baked sea bream, once a Christmas dish.

Modern times have seen feasting dishes such as wood-roasted *cochinillo*, tender suckling pig, or *cordero*, roast lamb (often on the bone) become everyday specialities. Likewise *jamón serrano* or *Iberico,* thinly sliced cured ham, is a favourite *tapa*.

REGIONAL SPECIALITIES

Madrid has many restaurants specialising in food from the regions. Here are some dishes to look out for on menus of all kinds. Andalucía's most famous speciality is *gazpacho,* a chilled garlicky raw tomato soup to which chopped garnishes and croutons are added to taste. It's extremely refreshing on hot summer days and has inspired many modern avant-garde variants.

From Valencia comes one of Spain's great dishes. Paella is named after the flat metal pan in which rice is cooked with either meat or fish – traditionally not both together – plus garlic, saffron and peppers. Spaniards think of paella, and other rice dishes *(arroces)*, as lunchtime dishes.

Fabada, from Asturias, is a variation on Madrid's *cocido,* but is cooked with velvety white faba beans and regional charcuterie like black sausage and chorizo. *Trucha a la navarra*, grilled trout

---

⊙ CHOCOLATE CON CHURROS

It is a Madrileño custom to finish a late night with *chocolate con churros* (hot chocolate with deep-fried loops of batter). Try the following establishments:

Chocolatería San Ginés, Pasadizo San Ginés 7, 24 hours; https://chocolateriasangines.com

Chocolatería Muñiz, Calle de Calatrava 3; 24 hours

San Miguel market at night

stuffed with a slice of ham, is a speciality of Navarra, while from Galicia there's *caldo gallego*, a rich vegetable soup.

A wide variety of sophisticated fish dishes come from the Basque country. Try *bacalao al pil pil* (salt cod in hot garlic sauce), *merluza a la vasca* (hake in a casserole with a thick sauce) or an extravagant luxury, *angulas a la bilbaína* (eels in a spicy olive oil and garlic sauce).

DRINKS

Wine menus today generally offer bottles from many Spanish denominations of origin: La Rioja, Navarra, Ribera del Duero, Jumilla, Somontano and Madrid are among the most popular. Also try cava, sparkling wine from Catalonia – Spain's answer to champagne.

If you just say *tinto* (red) or *blanco* (white) when asked for your choice of *vino*, you'll be given the house wine, which may come in a glass, bottle or be decanted into a jug. This is usually a reliable, budget choice. Many Spanish diners use a little sparkling mineral water or lemonade (*casera*) to dilute wine, especially in summer.

Spanish beers, in bottles or on draught (*caña*), are generally light and refreshing. *Sangría* is prepared in some Madrid bars and all will prepare *clara*, a beer and lemonade shandy. Sherry (*Jerez*), from Jerez de la Frontera in Andalucia, is delicious when well kept. Pale, dry *fino* is drunk chilled as an apéritif and also with soup and fish courses, while the rich, dark *oloroso* or PX is a good digestif. Spanish brandy varies: in this case you get what you pay for. Other spirits, made under licence in Spain, are often cheaper than imported labelled spirits and are served very generously.

Coffee is popular and is generally served black (*solo*), with a spot of milk (*cortado),* with hot milk (*con leche*) or with hot water (*americano).*

OPENING HOURS, PAYMENT AND PRICES

Note that many restaurants close for at least one day a week, often Sunday evening and all day Monday. Old-fashioned and family businesses also close for some or all of August and currently many bars close between lunch and dinner.

For payment, you may need cash: many places do not accept all credit cards and some do not accept any. Remember that for tapas, as well as meals, you generally pay at the end.

Curiously, Michelin-starred eating offers some of the best value if you look at set-menu prices, which may be half of those in northern European capitals.

Cocktail hour

⊙ TAPAS AND EL TAPEO

Tapas – the snacks for which Spanish bars and cafés are best known – are among Spain's great contributions to world cuisine.

The list of tapas available is almost endless, but some of the more common options include *aceitunas* (olives), *chorizo* (cured sausage), *champiñones* (mushrooms, usually fried in garlic), *queso* (cheese), *albóndigas* (meatballs), *croquetas* (croquettes of fish or chicken), *morcilla* (blood sausage), and the classic *tortilla española*, an omelette with potatoes fried in olive oil until golden.

A small plate is called a *tapa;* a larger serving, meant to be shared, is a *ración;* and half of this, a *media-ración*. To substitute for a conventional main course, choose perhaps three different items. Bars specialising in tapas are places where tapas grazing *(el tapeo)* is the order of the day. Two good central areas are La Latina and Huertas, but there are good bars everywhere. Bear in mind that these days *tapas* are rarely free, and do not come cheap.

More than two centuries old, with bulls' heads and other taurine memorabilia on the walls, **Taberna de Antonio Sánchez** (Mesón de Paredes 13; www.tabernaantoniosanchez.com) is legendary. **Taberna Almendro 13** (Calle Almendro 13) is a great corner bar specialising in *fino* and *manzanilla* (dry sherry) and serving a wide variety of tapas and *raciones* to a noisy local crowd. **Casa del Labra** (Calle de Tetuán 12; www.casalabra.es) is a great old spot near the Puerta del Sol, where the Socialist party was founded, and still serves homemade salt-cod *croquetas* and *soldados de Pavia* (saltcod fried in batter). More sophisticated is **Bocaito** (Calle de la Libertad 6), which serves stylish Andalusian *tapas* from its double-sided bar.

TO HELP YOU ORDER...

Could we have a table ¿**Nos puede dar una mesa, por favor?**
Do you have a set menu? **¿Hay un menú del día?**
The menu, please **La carta, por favor**
The bill, please **La cuenta, por favor**
I'd like a/an/some... **Me gustaría pedir...**

THE BASICS...

beer **cerveza/caña**
bread **pan**
cutlery **los cubiertos**
dessert **postre**
fish **pescado**
fruit **fruta**
glass **vaso/copà**
ice cream **helado**
meat **carne**
mineral water **agua mineral**

napkin **servilleta**
plate **plato**
potatoes **patatas**
rice **arroz**
salad **ensalada**
sandwich **bocadillo**
sugar **azúcar**
tea **té**
water (chilled) **agua (fresca)**
wine **vino**

...AND READ THE MENU

albondigas meatballs
almejas clams
anchoas anchovies
atún/bonito tuna
calamares squid
cangrejo crab
caracoles snails
cerdo pork
chuleta chop/cutlet
cordero lamb
entremeses hors d'oeuvres
gambas prawns

judías beans
langosta spiny lobster
lechón/cochinillo suckling pig
mariscos shellfish
ostras oysters
pimiento bell pepper
pollo chicken
pulpo octopus
ternera veal
trucha trout
verduras vegetables

PLACES TO EAT

The restaurant categories below reflect the cost of a three-course meal (starter, main course and dessert) plus a glass of house wine. Tax (IVA) is not included. 'L' means lunch, 'D' stands for dinner. At lunchtime, however, the majority of restaurants offer inexpensive two- or three-course fixed-priced menus (*menú del día* or *menú de la casa*), usually with two or three options for each course, making this, the main meal of the day, extremely affordable.

€€€€	over 50 euros
€€€	35–50 euros
€€	20–35 euros
€	below 20 euros

PLAZA MAYOR AND LA LATINA

Botín €€€ *Calle de Cuchilleros 17, tel: 91-366 4217. Open daily all year for L and D, www.botin.es.* Botín claims to be world's oldest continuously running restaurant, having opened in 1725. Many clients are visitors to the city, but Spaniards are fans too. The nooks and crannies of the old dining rooms are appealing. The roast suckling pig and roast leg of lamb prepared in wood ovens give a great taste of traditional Castilian cooking.

Casa Lucío €€€ *Cava Baja 35, tel: 91-365 8217. Open daily L and D. Closed Aug, www.casalucio.es.* A famous cave-like tavern with hanging cured hams, popular with affluent locals and visitors alike. High-quality Castilian cuisine: specialities include their legendary eggs with cured ham (*huevos estrellados*).

Casa Paco €€€ *Puerta Cerrada 11, tel: 913 663 167. Open Mon–Sat L and D, Sun L only, www.casapaco1933.es.* A classic, 85-year-old eatery serving up beef, priced by weight, seared and usually served very pink, grilled fish and, downstairs in the bar, cheese and cured ham. Attracts a stylish crowd.

Julián de Tolosa €€€€ *Cava Baja 18, tel: 91-365 8210. Open Mon–Sat L and D, Sun L only,* https://juliandetolosa.com. Superb plain Basque cooking: the huge charcoal-grilled rib steaks (*chuletón*) for two are a star dish, but the hake, black beans and red peppers are also good. Pricy but a great dining experience.

HUERTAS, SANTA ANA AND LAVAPIÉS

Taberna La Alhambra € *Calle Victoria 9, tel: 91-521 0708. Open daily for L and D.* Decoratively tiled bar on a side street near Plaza Santa Ana. Established in 1929, it serves great Andalusian cooking, simple but well done. *Apéritivos* are free with drinks and the main dishes, from paella to fried goat's cheese, are good at fair prices.

Casa Alberto €€ *Calle de las Huertas 18, tel: 91-429 9356. Open Tue–Sat for L and D, Sun L only,* www.casaalberto.es. An 1827 tavern where Cervantes legendarily lived, this is a good place for *tapas* and beer pulled from an antique tap, or a sit-down meal. Meatballs, salt cod with red peppers and beef fillet are good choices.

Cervecería Alemana €–€€ *Plaza Santa Ana 6, tel: 91-429 7033. Open Wed–Mon for L and D. Closed Aug,* www.cerveceriaalemana.com. Whatever the service and food are like – both could be improved – this place is unmissable for some because of its connections with Hemingway. There's a good range of beers and an acceptable choice of homemade *tapas* and *raciones* (bigger portions). Food served until 2am at weekends.

La Musa de Espronceda €–€€ *Sta Isabel 17, tel: 91-539 1284. Open Tue–Sat L and D, Sun L only.* A short stroll from the Reina Sofía, this buzzy young bar-restaurant serves great set-lunches and creative Basque-style *tapas*, called *pinchos*, until past midnight to an arts crowd. Friday and Saturday evenings see up to fifty choices laid out on the bar. Excellent service.

PALACIO REAL AND OPERA

La Bola €€ *Calle de la Bola 5, tel: 91-547 6930. Open Mon–Sat for L and D, Sun L only,* www.labola.es. This tiny, bright red restaurant on the corner of Calle de la Bola is a Madrid institution for its *cocido*, cooked in individual earthenware pots. Good shellfish and grilled meats and fish, too. Wonderful atmosphere. No credit cards.

Café de Oriente €–€€ *Plaza de Oriente 2, tel: 91-541 3974. Open daily for L and D*, www.cafedeoriente.es. Staying open late (the café serves until 1.30am Mon–Thu and Sun, and until 2.30am Fri–Sat), this brasserie is in a great location next to the Opera House, with summer terrace. Classic international cooking. Good for a late coffee or drink.

Cornucopia €€ *Calle Navas de Tolosa 9, tel: 91-521 3896. Open daily for L and D*, www.restaurantecornucopia.com. This elegant restaurant serves excellent, beautifully presented modern world cooking. Lovely desserts, homemade bread and bargain lunchtime set menu.

Taberna del Alabardero €€€ *Calle Felipe V 4–6, tel: 91-547 2577. Open daily for L and D*, www.grupolezama.es. This classic tavern is a good place to visit after a night at the opera or for a rejuvenating lunch after touring the Palacio Real. It's a bustling *tapas* bar at the front and, at the back, a more select Basque restaurant serving fresh fish and exquisite meat dishes till midnight.

SOL, GRAN VIA AND CHUECA

Artemisa € *Ventura de la Vega 4 and Tres Cruces 4, tel: 91-429 5092 and 91-521 8721. Open daily for L and D*, www.restaurantesvegetarianosar temisa.com. A good central vegetarian option, with two branches near the Prado and Gran Vía, serves creative dishes with very fresh ingredients. The lunch menu is very popular with nearby office workers. Rustic decor. Good wines, some organic.

Bocaito €€ *Calle de la Libertad 4–6, tel: 91-532 1219. Open Mon–Sat L and D, Sun L only. Closed Aug*; http://bocaito.com. One of the city's best traditional *tapas* bars, in the heart of Chueca. You can assemble a meal from the great *tapas* including croquettes, garlic prawns and octopus, or try the main courses in the restaurant, behind the double bar, featuring Castilian and Andalusian specialities.

Home Burger € *Calle de Silva 25, tel: 91-115 1279. Mon–Thu 1.30–4pm, 8.30pm–midnight, Fri and Sat 1.30–5pm, 8.30pm–midnight, Sun 1.30–5pm, 8.30–11pm,* www.homeburgerbar.com. A small chain of organic burger bars offering simple gourmet variations like different cheese toppings, good wine and real chips.

Lhardy €€€€ *Carrera de San Jerónimo 8, tel: 91 521 3385. Open Mon–Sat for L and D, Sun L only,* www.lhardy.com. Founded in 1839, Lhardy is part of Madrid's history, with formal 19th-century dining rooms upstairs and below a deli and *tapas* bar where you can enjoy pastries and consommé. The *cocido* is famous.

La Pecera del Círculo de Bellas Artes €€ *C/ Alcalá 42, tel: 91 360 5400;* www.lapeceradelcirculo.com. *Open all day daily (till 3am Fri and Sat).* Think huge chandeliers, marble statues and vast windows with lovely views onto Alcalá. The set lunch is the best option at this restaurant-café, but there is a great atmosphere. Beautiful summer terrace.

La Terraza del Casino €€€€ *Alcalá 15, tel: 91-532 1275. Open Tue–Sat L and D,* www.casinodemadrid.es. Paco Roncero's avant-garde yet personalised cooking in the El Bullí school draws a stylish crowd to this grand dining room. Great wines and service.

Zara €€ *Calle Barbieri 8, tel: 91-532 2074. Open Tue–Sat L and D. Closed Aug,* www.restaurantezara.com. For something different, try this packed restaurant serving Cuban beans, stews and daiquiris in a genuine family atmosphere. You may need to queue (it's worth it).

SALAMANCA, CASTELLANA AND PRADO

Café Gijón €€€ *Paseo de Recoletos 21, tel: 91-521 5425. Open 7am–2am daily,* www.cafegijon.com. Legendary literary café fashionable with arty types since it opened in 1888. It still serves as a meeting place at any time of day, for a coffee or drink, lunch or supper. Two set-price menus or à la carte.

Diverxo €€€€ *Calle Padre Damian 23, Eurobuilding, tel: 91-570 0766. Open Tue–Sat,* www.diverxo.com. Currently rated as Madrid's top avant-garde kitchen, producing four tasting menus adapted to each table's tastes. The dozen or so dishes in each are beautiful to the eye and explore intriguing global flavours. Booking by email (info@ diverxo.com) advised a month in advance.

Étimo €€€ *Calle de Ayala 27, tel: 91-375 9883. Open Tue–Sat L and D,* http://etimo.es. This new restaurant run by acclaimed chef Begoña Fraire serves up predominantly Spanish fare. The menu changes seasonally and is based on local seasonal products. Its four- or five-course menus are worth a try.

Etxegarate €€ *Calle Zurbano 43, tel: 91-319 9025. Open daily L and D,* www.etxegarate.com. Etxegarate specialises in simple Spanish food. The excellent, affordable menu of the day (€13) is a must. If you like tortillas and pintxos, there's plenty to choose from here.

Santceloni €€€€ *Paseo de la Castellana, 57, tel: 91-210 8840. Open Mon–Fri L and D, Sat D, closed Aug and Holy Week,* www.restaurantesantceloni.com. Madrid's most stylish hotel restaurant, masterminded by the late Catalan star-chef Santi Santamaría, with excellent tasting menus that strike the perfect balance between tradition and creativity, plus a cheese trolley to die for. Good wines and fine service.

Sanxenxo €€€€ *Ortega y Gasset 40, tel: 91-577 8272. Open Mon–Sat L and D,* www.combarro.com. Superb fish and shellfish flown in daily from Spain's four coasts, cooked simply to showcase the premier quality. If you love shellfish this place is worth every penny.

OUTSIDE MADRID
Ávila

El Molino de la Losa €€€ *Bajada de la Losa 12, tel: 920-211 102. Open daily for L and D, closed Sun D, closed Nov–Apr,* www.elmolinodelalosa. com. Enjoy great views from this ancient mill on an island in the river. Classic and modern cuisine.

San Lorenzo El Escorial

El Charolés €€€ *Calle Floridablanca 24, tel: 91-890 5975. Open daily for L and D, closed Christmas Eve and New Year's Eve,* www.charolesrestaurante.com. Inventive market cooking and a comprehensive wine list. Serves *cocido* on Wednesday and Friday, except for fiesta days. Luscious lemon and honey ice cream.

Segovia

Mesón de Cándido €€–€€€ *Plaza Azoguejo 5, tel: 921-425 911. Open daily for L and D,* www.mesondecandido.es. This family-run restaurant in the shadow of the aqueduct has been an inn since the 18th century and was made a national monument in 1941. Legendary wood-roast meats.

El Cardenal €€€ *Paseo Recaredo 24, tel: 925-220 862. Open daily for L and D,* www.haciendadelcardenal.com. The restaurant at the lovely Hacienda del Cardenal has long been one of Toledo's top kitchens. Best known for its wood roasts. Delightful summer terrace.

Restaurante José María €€€ *Cronista Lecea 11, tel: 921-461 111. Open daily for L and D,* www.restaurantejosemaria.com. A good stop whether you're just peckish or absolutely starving as there's a busy *tapas* bar at the front, as well as a relaxed restaurant. Try Segovian roasts or excellent Atlantic fish dishes.

Toledo

Restaurante Adolfo €–€€ *Calle Hombre de Palo 7, tel: 925-227 321. Open Mon–Sat for L and D, Sun L only,* www.grupoadolfo.com. Toledo haute cuisine is served in a medieval building near the cathedral. Game is a speciality here; the huge wine cellar is the city's finest.

A–Z TRAVEL TIPS

A SUMMARY OF PRACTICAL INFORMATION

A

ACCOMMODATION

Spanish hotels are rated by a star system, with five-star deluxe the top grade. The classifications often seem arbitrary; some two- and three-star places will be of the same quality as a hotel with a higher rating. About two-thirds of the city's hotels fall into the three- and four-star categories. Breakfast (usually a continental-style buffet) is rarely included in the room rate.

> I'd like a double/single room. **Me gustaría pedir una habitación doble/sencilla**
> with/without bath/shower **con/sin baño/ducha**
> double bed **cama matrimonial**
> What's the rate per night? **¿Cuál es el precio por noche?**
> Is breakfast included? **¿Está incluído el desayuno?**

Hotel reservation desks are found at Barajas Airport, at Chamartín and Atocha railway stations, and in the Torre de Madrid on Plaza de España. Before taking a room, the guest fills out a form, which states the hotel category, room number and price, and signs it. Winter months (Nov–Mar) are formally the low season, but in practice prices often vary through the year, between weekends and weekdays, and according to booking levels.

AIRPORT

Barajas Adolfo Suárez International Airport (MAD, www.aena.es), 12km (7.5 miles) northeast of Madrid, handles domestic and international flights. Currently Terminals 1, 2 and 4 are for international flights (Terminal 1 handles most charter flights, plus Easyjet and Ryanair; Terminal 2 operates Air France and KLM flights; Terminal 4 handles

Iberia, British Airways, Avianca and American Airlines). Terminal 4 also services the Barcelona Air Shuttle and Spanish regional carriers.

Coming through Arrivals *(Llegadas)* is quick; leaving through Departures *(Salidas)* is slow – allow plenty of time.

Taxis are available outside all terminals and cost €20-30 (cheaper rate applies if the distance covered is under 10km). Generally allow 20–30 minutes to reach the city centre. The cheaper, equally reliable option is the 24-hour Autobús Express Aeropuerto (www.emtmadrid. es), travelling either way in 30–40 minutes, with central drop-off and pick-up points at Plaza de Cibeles and Atocha railway station (charge €5). Alternatively, take urban bus no. 200 (€1.50) to Avenida de America where you can switch to metro or other buses.

Another inexpensive option, useful when traffic is heavy, is the Metro from the airport to Nuevos Ministerios station north of the city centre (journey time about 14 minutes). From here a change to Line 10 takes you to Plaza de España in about 15 minutes. A single ticket costs €4.50–5. Alternatively, buy a 10-in-one ticket, or *Abono*, for around €12, plus the airport supplement. Trains run from 6am–midnight. A modern train from T4 takes just 11 minutes to get to the city centre.

B

BICYCLE RENTAL

Although Madrid has few cycle lanes, travelling by bicycle through the parks, pedestrianised streets and old quarter's quiet lanes is safe and pleasant, especially in good weather. Among various companies that offer bicycles for hire, Trixi (www.trixi.com) is very central and also offers tours and skateboards.

BUDGETING FOR YOUR TRIP

There are numerous ways to save money by planning ahead. Flight prices may be a quarter of the price midweek. Local transport services and the municipal, royal and regional tourist bodies make changing offers that are worth researching ahead of time. These include flat-price tickets for limitless metro and rail travel and cut-price long-distance rail travel rates for advance booking. Buying the Paseo del Arte card gives you single entry to the three main museums of the city: the Prado, the Museo Reina Sofía and the Thyssen-Bornemisza. It costs around €30 and is valid for one year.

By sticking to the excellent set-menus offered by bars and restaurants you can keep your food expenses to a fixed budget.

C

CAMPING

Madrid has an excellent year-round camping site a short metro or bus ride east of the city, at Alameda de Osuna. Camping Osuna, Jardines de Aranjuez 1, tel: 91-741 0510, metro Canillejas / El Capricho (www.campingosuna.com), rents spaces for tents and caravans. Facilities include a good bar-restaurant and small supermarket.

CAR HIRE

To hire a car in Spain, you must usually be at least 21 years of age, with either an international driving licence or a valid licence (held at least for a year) from your own country. All motorcycle riders must wear helmets and ride with their headlights on, even during the day. Car hire must be paid for with a major credit card unless you leave a large deposit. Third-party insurance will be included; fully comprehensive may cost extra.

Cars can be hired per day with an additional fee according to mileage, or in package deals for a set number of days at unlimited mileage. The average daily cost for a middle-range car (Peugeot 306) with unlimited mileage and full insurance is around €40–60.

Car hire agencies include:

Enterprise Pl de España (carpark), tel: 915-425 015; www.enterprise.es

Avis Gran Vía 60, tel: 902-103 739; www.avis.es
Europcar Pa Atocha, Railway Station, tel: 911-505 000; www.europcar.es
Hertz Pl de España, C/ Princesa 14, tel: 915-425 805; www.hertz.es
Sixt Rda de Atocha 10, tel: 902-491 616; www.sixt.es

CLIMATE

You'd be wise to avoid Madrid in July and August, as many *Madrileños* do, unless you like stifling heat. Many restaurants and sites of interest close completely. In the winter months, Madrid can be very cold at times, too, with sub-zero temperatures, snow, and icy winds.

Spring, early summer and autumn are the best seasons to travel to Madrid – you're likely to experience ideal temperatures, low humidity and some of the brightest sunshine in Europe.

CLOTHING

Madrid's traditional smartness of dress has relaxed. Businessmen often wear an open-collar shirt in summer. But resort wear would be inappropriate in this big city and attracts stares when worn by the unwary. A few upper-echelon restaurants require jackets and ties for men. On visits to churches, it's best to wear modest cover-up clothing though in the heat of summer, no one is likely to prohibit men from entering in walking shorts.

CRIME AND SAFETY

Though Madrid is no more dangerous than any other capital city, tourists should be on guard, especially close to the Prado (where scams are often perpetrated), the Rastro, Gran Vía, Puerta del Sol, Plaza Mayor, Plaza de Toros bullring, on the Metro or at any large street gathering. The most common crimes are pickpocketing and the snatching of passports and handbags.

As ever, it pays to be careful. Do not leave luggage unattended; don't carry more money on your person than you'll need for daily expenses;

use the hotel safe deposit for larger sums and valuables; in crowds around street attractions and sports events, be on your guard against pickpockets; reject offers of flowers or other objects from street pedlars – they may be after your wallet; don't leave valuables in view inside your car, even when it's locked; photocopy personal documents and leave the originals in your hotel.

I want to report a theft. **Quiero denunciar un robo**
My ticket/wallet/passport/purse has been stolen. **Me han robado mi billete/cartera/pasaporte/monadera**

If you are robbed, contact the local police station or dial 092 for the city police *(policía municipal)*.

D

DRIVING

Crossing the border into Spain, you won't be asked for documents, but in the event of any problem you will have to produce your passport, driving licence, registration papers and insurance documents, which must be carried with you at all times when driving.

Cruce peligroso Dangerous crossroads
Curva peligrosa Dangerous bend
Despacio Slow
Peligro Danger
Prohibido adelantar No overtaking (passing)
Prohibido aparcar No parking
Sentido único One way (street)

Avoid driving in Madrid. Nerve-wracking traffic jams are a way of life, although there is a lull between 3.00 and 4.30pm. There are many accidents on the streets in the early hours of the morning, when the clubs close.

Rules and regulations. You should display a nationality sticker on your car. Most fines for traffic offences are payable on the spot or at a bank within a set time limit. Driving rules are the same throughout Spain: drive on the right, overtake (pass) on the left, yield right of way to vehicles coming from the right (unless your road is marked as having priority). Front and rear seat belts are compulsory.

Speed limits are 120kmh (75mph) on motorways, 100kmh (62mph) on broad main roads (two lanes each way), 90kmh (56mph) on other main roads, 50kmh (31mph), or as marked, in densely populated areas.

If you need help. Garages are efficient, but repairs may take time in busy areas. Spare parts are readily available for Spanish-built cars and many other popular models. For less-common makes, they may have to be imported. In an emergency, tel: 091.

E

ELECTRICITY

The standard electric current is 220 volts, but some hotels have a voltage of 110–120 in bathrooms as a safety precaution. Check before plugging in any appliance. Sockets (outlets) take round, two-pin plugs, so you will probably need an international adapter plug.

EMBASSIES AND CONSULATES

Many Western European countries have embassies in Madrid. Some useful addresses are as follows:

Australia: Torre Espacio, Paseo de la Castellana 259d, tel: 91-353 6600; www.spain.embassy.gov.au

Canada: Torre Espacio, Paseo de la Castellana 259d, tel: 91-382 8400; www.canadainternational.gc.ca

Ireland: Paseo de la Castellana 46, tel: 91-436 4093; www.dfa.ie/irish-embassy/Spain

New Zealand: Calle del Pinar 7, 3rd floor, tel: 91-523 0226; www.nzembassy.com

UK: Torre Espacio, Paseo de la Castellana 259d, tel: 91-714 6300; www.gov.uk/world/organisations/british-embassy-madrid (NB: Citizens of Commonwealth countries may apply to the UK embassy)

United States: Calle de Serrano 75, tel: 91-587 2200; https://es.usembassy.gov/embassy-consulates/madrid

EMERGENCIES (see also Health and medical care and Police)

In the event of an emergency, contact the relevant source of assistance:

Coordinated Emergency Number 112
Emergency Medical Care 112
Ambulance 061 or 901 222 222 (Red Cross/Cruz Roja)
City Police 092
National Police 091
Guardia Civil 062
Fire Service (Madrid) 080

G

GETTING THERE (see also Airport and Driving)

By Air. Madrid's airport Barajas is linked by daily non-stop flights from across Europe. Most flights from the US and Canada are direct; others stop first in Lisbon, Frankfurt or London. From Australia and New Zealand, regular one-stop flights go directly to Madrid.

There are direct flights to Madrid from the UK via British Airways (www.ba.com) and Iberia (www.iberia.es), as well as low-cost Easyjet (www.easyjet.com) and Ryanair (www.ryanair.com) flights from airports outside London. There are services between Madrid and the United States with Iberia, Delta and American Airlines (www.aa.com).

Domestic services are operated by Iberia (tel: 901-111 500), Vueling (tel: 0203 514 3971) and Ryanair (www.ryanair.com).

By Road. The main access road from France to Madrid skirts the western end of the Pyrenees. A motorway (expressway) runs from Biarritz (France) through the Basque Country via Bilbao to Burgos, from where you take the E25 motorway straight down to Madrid, 240km (150 miles) away.

Express coach services operate between London and Madrid as well as between other European cities and Madrid. For further details, visit www.eurolines.eu.

By Rail. Anyone travelling from the UK should take the Eurostar to Paris, from where there are overnight trains to Madrid. For discounts and special rail tickets, see page 132.

GUIDES AND TOURS

The Centro de Turismo de Madrid (City Tourism Office, Plaza Mayor 27, tel: 91-578 7810; daily 9.30am–9.30pm; www.esmadrid.com) offers personal advice, a database and historical and cultural tours by bus and on foot throughout the year, covering a wide array of topics and sights. Unless there's a large English-speaking group, though, tours are conducted in Spanish. Madrid City Tour (https://madrid.city-tour.com) organises hop-on, hop-off multi-language city bus tours that depart from the Prado daily Nov–Feb 10am–6pm, Mar–Oct 9am–10pm.

There are three main companies organising coach tours to Aranjuez, El Escorial, Toledo, Ávila and Segovia:

Viator, tel: 917 918 233, es.viator.com

Trapsatur San Bernardo 5–7 (Metro: Santo Domingo), tel: 91-541 6321, www.trapsatur.es

Insider's Madrid Manuela Malasaña 21 (Metro: Bilbao), tel: 699 493 193, www.insidersmadrid.com

H

HEALTH AND MEDICAL CARE

Standards of hygiene are high, and medical care in Madrid is excellent. Most doctors speak sufficient English to deal with foreign patients. The water is safe to drink, but bottled water is always safest, and is available everywhere. Most local people drink bottled water, *agua con gas* (carbonated) or *sin gas* (still). It is good, clean and inexpensive.

Visitors from EU countries with corresponding health-insurance facilities are entitled to medical and hospital treatment under the Spanish social security system. You must have your European Health Insurance Card (EHIC) card with you for reciprocal health care. Before travelling, British subjects should obtain an EHIC card (forms available at post offices, online at www.ehic.org.uk, or tel: 0845 606 2030).

It is recommended that you also take out reputable private medical insurance, which will be part of almost all travel insurance packages.

Chemists *(farmacias)* operate as a first line of defence for Spaniards, as pharmacists can prescribe drugs and are usually adept at making on-the-spot diagnoses. Pharmacies, marked by a green neon cross lit up when open, operate during normal business hours and one in every district remains open all night and on holidays. The location and phone number of this *farmacia de guardia* is posted on the door of all the other pharmacies. All-night pharmacies can also be contacted by calling 098. To locate a hospital or report a medical emergency, dial 112.

If you take drugs on prescription, ensure that you take extra supplies with you. Spanish chemists do not honour foreign prescriptions. Given the dry climate and sun levels, it is a good idea to wear sunscreen and carry water with you in both summer and winter.

L

LANGUAGE

After Chinese and English, the most widely spoken language in the world is Spanish, from Madrid to Manila, from Ávila to Argentina. The

Castilian spoken in Madrid is understood in most areas of Spain, although Catalan, Basque, Gallego and Valencian are official languages in their home areas. It's certainly worth learning a few basic phrases and the *Insight Spanish Phrasebook and Dictionary* covers all situations you are likely to encounter in your travels in Spain.

LGBTQ TRAVELLERS

Madrid has a vibrant LGBTQ scene, which is centred in the neighbourhood of Chueca, whose grid of narrow lanes lies just north of the Gran Vía. The local multitude of bars and clubs vary from low-key to hardcore, and magazines on gay social life, such as *Shangay* (https://shangay.com), give further information. This *barrio's* small café-lined central square is a hive of hetero-LGBTQ activity during the summer and is a good place to meet people.

Gay Pride week, at the end of June, includes a high-heels race and a Saturday procession with floats that is a hugely popular fiesta with young and old alike, bringing the city centre to a standstill.

M

MAPS

A free street map covering the whole of Madrid is available at Tourist Information Offices at the airport, railway stations and in the city. It is sufficient for virtually all city travel. Visitors should also pick up the pocket-sized map of the Metro underground system *(un plano del metro)*, available free at any Metro station.

MEDIA

Television. There are several nationwide television channels in Spain: TVE-1, La 2 (public), Cuatro, La Sexta, Antena 3 and Tele 5. Many hotels offer Canal Plus and its linked channels. In Madrid, you can also watch Telemadrid, which often offers the dual option of watching films in their original language.

Most programmes are in Spanish with the occasional late-night film in the original language. Many hotels have access to a wider range of satellite stations.

Print media. The Spanish quality national daily papers (*periódicos*) sold in Madrid include *El País, La Vanguardia, ABC* and *El Mundo*. They provide full local information on cinema, theatre, regular and satellite television programming, and list chemist shops that are open late at night. *El Mundo* includes handy supplements with its Friday edition, giving listings on exhibitions, art shows and film schedules, along with lists of restaurants, entertainment and television. El País publishes a similar supplement on Friday, called *Tentaciones*. These are along the lines of the weekly, all-encompassing *Guía del Ocio (Guide to Leisure)*.

You will also be able to find *the International New York Times* and *Time* and *Newsweek* magazines at major newsstands. Other papers, such as *The Times, Guardian* and *Wall Street Journal*, can be purchased at larger stands, particularly around the Puerta del Sol.

MONEY

The currency of Spain is the euro, which comes in coins valued 1 euro, 2 euros, plus 50, 20, 10, 5, 2 and 1 cents. Bills are in denominations of 5,

Where's the nearest bank/currency exchange office?**¿Dónde está el banco/la casa de cambio más cercana?**

I want to change some pounds/dollars. **Quiero cambiar libras/dólares.**

Do you accept travellers cheques? **¿Aceptan cheques de viajero?**

Can I pay with a credit card? **¿Se puede pagar con tarjeta?**

How much is that? **¿Cuánto es?**

10, 20, 50, 100, 200 and 500 euros.

Credit cards. These are used extensively in Spain and most towns have cashpoint facilities, which are generally the cheapest way to change cash, especially if you withdraw quantities of €200.

O

OPENING TIMES

The practice of the siesta, the long midday break and nap, is losing adherents in Madrid, except in the hot months. The big department stores and supermarkets remain open all day. Still, very few small shops remain open all day; their usual hours are from 9.30am–1.30 or 2pm and 4.30 or 5–8pm, Mon–Sat. Some shops close on Saturday afternoons. Increasingly, department stores and high street chain outlets open on Sundays. Major museums are now shifting to unbroken day-long opening.

Restaurants serve lunch from 1–4pm; in the evening their timing depends on the kind of customers they expect. Local people usually eat between 9 and 11pm or later. Places catering to foreigners may function from 7pm on, and many stay open throughout the day.

Banks are usually Mon–Fri 8.15 or 9am–2pm. Some banks such as La Caixa open on Thursday evening. All banks close on Saturday afternoon, Sunday and fiestas. Government offices and most businesses are open from 9am–2pm and from 3pm to anywhere from 5.30–7pm; summer hours mid-June to mid-Sept are 8am–3pm.

P

POLICE

Spanish municipal and national police are efficient, strict and courteous – and generally very responsive to issues involving foreign tourists. In Madrid, dial 092 for municipal police and 091 for national police. The central police station (Policía Nacional), with interpreters, is located at Calle Leganitos 19, near Plaza de España (tel: 91-548 7985).

POST OFFICES

Post offices *(correos)* are identified by yellow-and-white signs with a crown and the words 'Correos y Telégrafos'. District post offices open Mon–Fri 8.30am–8.30pm and Sat 8.30am–2pm. The central post office on Calle de Montalban 1/Paseo del Prado 1 is open Mon–Fri 8.30am–9.30pm, Sat until 2pm (tel: 91-523 0694). Most post offices close at 8.30pm, but El Corte Inglés has instore post offices open throughout their retailing hours including Sundays.

In postal addresses, note that s/n ('sin numero') means that the full address does not include a street number.

PUBLIC HOLIDAYS

1 January *Año Nuevo* New Year's Day
6 January *Epifanía* Epiphany
20 January *San Sebastián* St Sebastian's Day
1 May *Fiesta del Trabajo* Labour Day
25 July *Santiago Apóstol* St James's Day
15 August *Asunción* Assumption
12 October *Día de la Hispanidad* Discovery of America Day (Spanish National Day)
1 November *Todos los Santos* All Saints' Day
6 December *Día de la Constitución* Constitution Day
8 December *Inmaculada Concepción* Immaculate Conception
25 December *Navidad* Christmas Day
26 December *La Fiesta Navidad* Christmas Holiday
Moveable dates:
Jueves Santo Holy Thursday
Viernes Santo Good Friday
Lunes de Pascua Easter Monday
Corpus Christi Corpus Christi

In addition to these nationwide holidays, there are big celebrations in Madrid on 2 May (El Dos de Mayo), and public holidays on 15 May, the city's patron saint's day (San Isidro Labrador/St Isidore the Husbandman), and on 9 November, La Almudena.

R

RELIGION

The national religion of Spain is Roman Catholicism, and Mass is said regularly in the churches of Madrid. There are churches of most major faiths; the tourist information offices have information on religious services, including those in foreign languages. Note that many churches open only for Mass.

T

TELEPHONES

Spain's country code is 34. Madrid's local area code, 91, must be dialled before all phone numbers, even for local calls. To make a direct overseas call, first dial 00 and then dial the country and city codes.

Mobile phone use in EU countries is now included in most monthly plans for no extra cost, but some restrictions and exceptions still apply. If in doubt, contact your local provider for more information before you travel.

The main international mobile operators in Spain are Vodafone, Orange and Yoigo. The main Spanish operator is Movistar. At mobile operators' city centre outlets you can buy SIM cards, seek technical help or buy pay-as-you-go phones which may be topped up at many shops and internet cafés.

You can also make direct-dial local and international calls from Telefónica's public phone booths (cabinas) in the street. Most operate with both coins and cards (tarjetas telefónicas), available from tobacconists. International telephone credit cards can also be used. Most bars have coin-operated or meter telephones available for public use as well. Post office telephones and internet bureaux known as *locutorios* are often the cheapest option.

TIME ZONES

Spanish time coincides with the rest of Western Europe – Greenwich Mean Time plus one hour. In spring, another hour is added for Daylight Saving Time (Summer Time).

TIPPING

Service is usually included in restaurant bills, but it is customary to leave the spare change in the dish when eating at a modest restaurant and a few cents at a bar. When dining at a fairly smart restaurant, an additional 5–10 percent of the bill is appropriate. Small change or a 10 percent tip is fine for an average taxi ride.

TOILETS

Toilet doors are distinguished by a 'C' for *Caballeros* (gentlemen) or 'S' for *Señoras* (ladies) or by a variety of pictographs (which are often amusing).

Where are the toilets? **¿Dónde están los servicios?**

TOURIST INFORMATION

UK: 1st floor, 100 George Street, W1U 8NU London; tel: 44 0207 317 2020; www.spain.info.
US: 2655 Le Jeune Rd (Gables International Plaza), Suite 605, Coral Gables, FL 33134 Miami, tel: 305-476 1966; Water Tower Place, Suite 915 East, 845 North Michigan Ave, Chicago, IL 60611, tel: 312 642 1992; 8383 Wilshire Blvd, Suite 960, 90211 Beverly Hills, CA 90211; tel: 323-658 7195; 60 East 42nd Street, Suite 5300 (53rd Floor), New

York, NY 10165-0039; tel: 212-265-8822; www.spain.info.

Canada: 2 Bloor St. West, Suite 3402, Toronto, Ontario M4W 3E2; tel: 1416-961 4079; www.spain.info.

In Spain:

Tourist information for all of Spain is available at the Madrid tourist offices *(oficinas de información turística)* in Barajas airport (T1 and 4 arrivals); at Duque de Medinaceli 2; in Chamartín station, Door 10; and in Atocha station, close to the AVE platforms. All open Mon–Fri 8 or 9am–7 or 8pm, Sat 9am–1 or 2pm.

The main Madrid city tourist office is at Plaza Mayor 27 (Casa de Panadería), tel: 91-578 7810, and is open daily 9.30am–9.30pm. There are information kiosks at the Santiago Bernabéu stadium in Plaza de Cibeles; Plaza de Callao; Centro Arte Reina Sofía and Plaza de Colón (underpass) and Plaza Neptuno. All except Plaza Cibeles (10am–8pm) and Santiago Bernabéu (8am–9.30pm) open at 9.30am and close at 8.30pm.

For telephone information on tourist facilities and practical matters, tel: 010 for the City Information Office.

TRANSPORT

Madrid has a reliable and comprehensive public transport system. Getting around town, especially by Metro (subway/tube) is easy, rapid, and inexpensive. Collect up-to-date Metro and train maps from station ticket offices. One website provides information for all services: https://www.crtm.es.

Buses *(autobuses)*. Inner-city buses currently operate a set fare regardless of the route or length of journey in the city centre. You enter from the front and pay the driver or stamp your multi-journey ticket. You don't need to have the exact fare, but you should offer coins. Press the buzzer at the stop you require and leave by the rear door.

An *Abono* is good for 10 journeys by bus or Metro and works out much cheaper than buying 10 individual tickets. It can be purchased from the bus information booths at Puerta del Sol, Plaza Callao, Plaza de la Cibeles and Plaza de Castilla, as well as in every Metro station.

If you are planning to spend an extended period of time in Madrid and doing a lot of bus and Metro travelling, purchase an Abono 30 días. This card can be applied for at any *estanco* by filling out a form and providing a passport-size photograph and a photocopy of your passport or national identity document. It is valid for a month, with reductions for people under 18 and over 65.

Buses are in service 6am–11.30pm. For municipal bus information, tel: 91-406 8800.

Metro. The Madrid Metro system is the fastest, cheapest and most efficient way of getting around the city. It operates from 6am–1.30am. Most trains have air-conditioning. Central journeys currently have flat-rate tickets and you can buy a cut-rate Abono, which allows you to make 10 trips (by Metro or bus) or a 1-, 2-, 3-, 5- or 7-day *Abono Turístico*. For information, tel: 012 or go to www.crtm. es. The ticket also entitles travel on urban buses, RENFE trains and metro ligero (trams).

Taxis. Madrid taxis are relatively inexpensive and plentiful. They are white, have a transversal red stripe on the sides and the Madrid coat of arms. They can be hailed with relative ease on main thoroughfares or may be found at *paradas de taxi* (taxi stands), indicated by a large white 'T' against a dark blue background, or requested by phone. They are available if they are displaying a green *libre* (free) sign on the windscreen or have a little green light on. If a red sign with the name of a Madrid neighbourhood is displayed, it means it is on its way home and not obliged to pick you up unless you are going in the same direction.

A meter on the dashboard indicates an initial fare at the start of the journey, and chalks up an extra sum for every kilometre. If you ask the driver to wait, he can charge you a set price per hour. Supplements can be added on Sunday and holidays; from 11pm–6am;

for pick-up or delivery at a railway station, football stadium or bull-ring; for pick-up or delivery at the race track, Club de Campo, or the Club Puerta de Hierro; for each piece of luggage; and for trips to or from the airport. If you leave the municipal limits for the suburbs, the driver is entitled to ask for double the fare per kilometer as of that point.

Trains *(trenes)*. Spanish trains have two classes: First *(Primera* or *1ª)* and Second *(Segunda* or *2ª)*, and a variety of categories, which vary in terms of comfort. The Talgo is a fast, comfortable train with video entertainment; the TERs and Electrotrens have similar facilities, but are not as fast. On night trains, one can usually get a cama (small, private compartment) or an inexpensive *litera* (a couchette in a compartment shared with five other passengers). *Rapidos* are local day trains good for short journeys. AVEs are high-speed bullet trains that form a good network around the country.

Madrid's northern railway station, **Chamartín**, at Avenida Pio XII in the north of the city, handles 80 percent of the city's rail traffic, including AVE services to Segovia and Valladolid. The station has a shopping and entertainment complex. The former Estación del Norte, now called **Príncipe Pío**, only operates trains to Alcalá de Henares. **Atocha** station in the south of the city operates AVE and other services to and from Andalucía, Castilla La Mancha, Extremadura and Levante (AVE journey times Seville or Malaga 2.5 hours, Toledo 30 minutes, Barcelona via Zaragoza 2.5 hours, Valencia 1 hour 40 minutes). There are shops, restaurants and left-luggage lockers (daily 5.30am–10.20pm).

When leaving Madrid by train, check your tickets carefully, as the Estrella express night trains leave from Chamartín rather than Atocha, and services to Levante (the East Coast, including Valencia and Alicante) leave from both Atocha and Chamartín.

Rail tickets. There are many ways to save money on rail travel in Spain. For more information see the website of the national rail company RENFE: tel: 902-320 320; www.renfe.com.

Visitors other than Europeans can buy a Eurail pass (www.eurail. com). It allows unlimited first or second-class travel throughout Spain and 30 other participating countries. These must be purchased before your arrival in Europe.

Europeans can take advantage of the Interrail scheme (www.inter rail.com) which permits unlimited second-class travel in up to 31 European countries.

If you don't have a Eurail or Interrail pass, you can buy a RENFE Spain pass offering 4–12 journeys during a calendar month at fixed prices.

It is worth asking the RENFE office about discounts for advance booking, especially by web, which rise to 60 percent for certain routes and trains. Ask at stations or see www.renfe.com for details.

When's the next train to...? **¿Cuándo sale el próximo tren para...?**
A ticket to... **Un billete para...**
single (one-way) **ida**
return (round-trip) **ida y vuelta**
What's the fare to...? **¿Cuánto es la tarifa a ...?**

V

VISAS AND ENTRY REQUIREMENTS

Visitors from the EU (and citizens of Andorra, Liechtenstein, Monaco and Switzerland) require only a valid national identity card from their home state to enter Spain. As British citizens have no identity cards, they need a passport. Citizens of the United States, Australia and New Zealand require a valid passport and are automatically authorised for a three-month stay. Visitors from elsewhere must obtain a visa from the Spanish consulate in their own country before setting off. Passport or identity card numbers are often required with flight bookings as a security measure.

Visitors can prolong a three-month stay for an additional three-month period by applying for an extension in Madrid at the Comisaría de Policía, Sección de Extranjería, Calle Los Madrazos 9.

In order to reside in Spain for an extended period, a Residencia (*Visado de Residencia Serie V*) must be obtained from the Spanish embassy or consulate in one's country of origin. EU nationals are allowed to live and work in Spain, but should check residency requirements with their nearest Spanish embassy before departure.

W

WEBSITES AND INTERNET ACCESS

There is free internet access in the Plaza Mayor tourist office, at the airport and numerous paying telephone and internet points (ask for a *locutorio*). Helpful websites are:

www.tourspain.es Site of Turespaña, the National Tourism Office.

www.esmadrid.com Madrid City Council's website, with links to transport and accommodation information.

www.patrimonionacional.es Website for numerous monuments, museums, parks and other sights owned by the Spanish royal family.

Y

YOUTH HOSTELS

Madrid has two youth hostels. They are Albergue Juvenil Richard Scherrmann (Casa de Campo; tel: 91-463 5699; 124 beds), and the Hat Madrid (Calle Imperial 9; tel: 91-772 85 72; www.thehatmadrid. com).

To make a booking you need an international albergues ID card. Rates are from €14–25 per person, for bed and breakfast, depending on your age.

RECOMMENDED HOTELS

Visitors to Madrid have plenty of choice with regard to where to stay in the city centre. Traditional *pensiones* (guesthouses) and *hostales* (modest, often family-owned hotels) are scattered around town. Palatial and boutique hotels are clustered in the main tourist areas: Puerta del Sol, Gran Vía, Paseo del Prado and Chueca. The following selection includes our top choices to cover a range of tastes. If you are staying in a very central hotel, particularly around the Gran Vía or Puerta del Sol, note that rooms facing onto the street can be very noisy at weekends. Interior rooms (*interiores*) may be darker, but also quieter. If you plan on staying out late you may like to check whether there is someone on the hotel reception 24 hours a day (usual, but not always the case). Wi-fi is usually available, but check first.

Most hotel rates do not include breakfast. Weekend rates and special deals are available at many hotels. Out-of-town rates can drop by up to 50 percent midweek. The rates quoted here are intended to give an indication of the cost of a double room in high season for one night.

€€€€	over 300 euros
€€€	200–300 euros
€€	100–200 euros
€	below 100 euros

SOL, PLAZA MAYOR, SANTA ANA

Cat's Hostel € *Calle Cañizares 6, tel: 91-369 2807;* www.catshostel. com. Cool young hostel with 200 beds in dormitories or double rooms grouped around a central Moorish patio, a basement bar and excellent location for alternative arts and nightlife.

Hostal Madrid € *Calle Esparteros 6, tel: 91-522 0060;* www.hostal-madrid.info. An extremely well-priced, quiet, central hostal, offering attractive, air-conditioned rooms and apartments, all with own bathrooms. Apartment 43 is particularly nice. Popular with a young crowd. 15 rooms and 4 apartments.

Hotel Me Madrid Reina Victoria €€€ *Plaza Santa Ana 14, tel: 91-701 6000;* www.melia.com. When the much-loved Reina Victoria was revamped, its cocktail bar and rooftop terrace and restaurant quickly became part of the smart Madrid scene. Hotel rooms are well fitted and the location is perfect for theatre, art galleries and nightlife. The decor and feel are glamorous.

Persal €–€€ *Plaza del Angel 12, tel: 91-369 4643;* www.hostalpersal. com. One of the best *hostales* in Madrid, Persal is set in a 19thcentury townhouse near the Plaza Mayor. Comfortable rooms. Friendly service. Buffet breakfast included.

Petit Palace Posada del Peine €€ *Calle Postas 17, tel: 91-523 8151;* www. petitpalace.com. Boutique hotel in the pedestrianised old town, just off the Plaza Mayor, combining a historic atmosphere with designer and hi-tech details. 71 rooms, all with their own iPad.

PALACIO REAL AND OPERA

Hotel Room Mate Mario €–€€ *Calle Campomanes 4, tel: 91-548 8548;* https://room-matehotels.com/es/mario. A great hotel on a quiet side street about one minute's walk from the Opera House. The 54 rooms are stylishly designed, with modern decor, all mod cons (including air conditioning) and good-sized bathrooms. Friendly staff. Lovely big buffet breakfast. One of four Room Mate Hotels in Madrid. Highly recommended.

GRAN VÍA, CHUECA, PLAZA DE ESPAÑA

Madrid Suites San Mateo € *Calle San Mateo 21-2º, tel: 91-448 5059;* https://madridsuitessanmateo.negocio.site. A lovely hotel with clean if small, simply furnished single, double and triple rooms. There is a small salon and outer rooms are all double glazed.

Iberostar Las Letras €€–€€€ *Gran Vía 11, tel: 91-523 7980;* www.hoteldelasletras.com. Spacious designer hotel, with a stylish mix of old and new decor. Facilities such as the library, urban spa, the rooftop terrace bar, popular with locals, and Japanese cuisine, offer comfort with a difference.

Hotel Liabeny €€ *Calle Salud 3, tel: 91-531 9000;* www.liabeny.es. Right in the centre of Madrid, this large affordable hotel offers 220 rooms of seven types. Buffet breakfast included. The hotel's Sensaciones restaurant serves up tasty Mediterranean and international dishes.

Hotel Madrid Plaza España €€ *Calle Gran Vía 74, tel: 91-547 0900;* www.melia.com. Large hotel in the heart of Madrid, within easy walking distance of major sites. Premium breakfast buffet. Fitness centre open 24 hours. 112 rooms.

Hotel Petit Palace Chueca €€ *Calle de Hortaleza 3, tel: 91-521 1043;* www.petitpalacechueca.com. A stylish small hotel at the southern end of Chueca's lively Calle de Hortaleza. Comfortable spacious rooms, with chic minimalist decor. 58 rooms.

Hotel Room Mate Óscar €€€ *Plaza Vázquez de Mella 12, tel: 91-701 1173;* https://room-matehotels.com/es/oscar. The rooftop swimming pool, pop decor and varied designer rooms at reasonable prices have put this on the map as Chueca's hippest hotel.

Hotel Santa Bárbara € *Plaza Santa Bárbara 4-3º, tel: 91-446 2345;* www.hostalsantabarbaramadrid.com. Bargain old-fashioned *hostal* just outside Chueca, with good Metro links from the airport and around the city.

SALAMANCA AND THE PRADO

Hotel Vincci SoMa €€ *Calle Goya 79, tel: 91-435 7545;* www.vinccihoteles.com. Chic four-star hotel with minimalist decor caters to the very cool crowd. It has a smart fitness suite and a hip restaurant. A classy choice, for Salamanca's upmarket shopping zone. 177 rooms.

Hotel Mora € *Paseo del Prado 32, tel: 91-420 1569;* www.hotelmora. com. Down the street from the Prado and the Botanical Garden, this medium-sized (62-roomed) 1930s hotel offers great value for money. Rooms are plain, but they are clean and airy. No groups permitted. Triple rooms are available. There's a busy cafeteria downstairs. Free Wifi and cable TV.

Hotel Unico €€€ *Claudio Coello 67, tel: 91-781 0173;* www.unicoho telmadrid.com. This boutique hotel situated along the city's Golden Mile is sleek and minimalist. It offers its guests the services of personal trainers and shoppers, a patio garden, fitness and wellness suites as well as luxurious en-suite rooms. The restaurant, with two Michelin stars, is in the hands of Catalan chef Ramón Freixa, and stays open all day Sunday.

Hotel Wellington €€€€ *Calle de Velázquez 8, tel: 91-575 4400;* www. hotel-wellington.com. This lavishly appointed hotel has hosted many celebrities from Ernest Hemingway to Matt Damon. It boasts a Michelin-starred Japanese restaurant, Kabuki Wellington, and a Basque restaurant, Goizeko Wellington. The facilities include a lovely rooftop garden, a large outdoor swimming pool and a wellness club. 250 rooms.

The Westin Palace €€€–€€€€ *Plaza de las Cortes 7, tel: 91-360 8000;* www.westinpalacemadrid.com. A palatial Belle Epoque hotel opposite Spain's Congress; the five-star, 467-roomed Palace is less formal than the Ritz, but still a chic institution. The hotel combines old-world glamour with a 24-hour business centre and fitness suite. Spectacular glass-roofed domed lounge.

OUTSIDE MADRID

Ávila

Parador de Ávila €€ *Marqués de Canales de Chozas 2, tel: 920-211 340;* www.parador.es. Paradores are state-run hotels, usually within renovated historic buildings. This one convincingly updates a 16th-century palace downstairs. Rooms are modern, but homely. Just within Ávila's walls. There's a good restaurant and summer terrace. 61 rooms.

Segovia

Parador de Segovia €–€€ *Carretera de Valladolid s/n, tel: 921-443 737; www.parador.es.* This 1970s state-owned parador has breathtaking views of the magical outline of Segovia, including the Roman aqueduct, medieval walls, cathedral and castle (all illuminated at night). Perched on a hill 3km (2 miles) north of the city, it's less convenient than hotels in the old quarter, but perfect if you've got some time to relax in Segovia. 113 rooms.

Toledo

Hotel Abad €–€€ *Real del Arrabal 1, tel: 925-283 500; www.hotelabad. com.* This stylishly decorated, three-star independent hotel has 22 rooms, each individually designed. It's set in an old blacksmith's shop; careful renovation has maintained original hand-hewn wooden ceilings. Half-price deals in low season.

Parador de Toledo €€–€€ *Cerro del Emperador, s/n, tel: 925-221 850; www.parador.es.* This is still the most popular hotel for groups. Built as a wooden *ligarrol*, or local farmstead, it has stunning views from the terraces and a large pool. Ten minutes' drive from the city. Reserve in advance. A good choice in summer.

Sercotel Hotel Pintor El Greco €–€€ *Calle Alamillos del Tránsito 13, tel: 925-285 191; www.hotelpintorelgreco.com.* This tastefully converted hotel in a 16th-century bakery is in the heart of the old Jewish quarter, next to the El Greco museum and synagogues. The sunny rooms surround a courtyard. Pets allowed. Good views. Breakfast only. 57 rooms.

DICTIONARY

ENGLISH–SPANISH

adj adjective   **adv** adverb   **BE** British English   **n** noun   **prep** preposition   **v** verb

A

abbey la abadía
accept v aceptar
access el acceso
accident el accidente
accommodation el alojamiento
account la cuenta
acupuncture la acupuntura
adapter el adaptador
address la dirección
admission la entrada
after después;
~**noon** la tarde;
~**shave** el bálsamo para después del afeitado
age la edad
agency la agencia
AIDS el sida
air el aire; ~
conditioning el aire acondicionado;
~**pump** el aire;
~**line** la compañía aérea; ~**mail** el correo aéreo; ~**plane** el avión; ~**port** el aeropuerto
aisle el pasillo; ~ **seat** el asiento de pasillo
allergic alérgico; ~
reaction la reacción alérgica

allow v permitir
alone solo
alter v (clothing) hacer un arreglo
alternate route el otro camino
aluminum foil el papel de aluminio
amazing increíble
ambulance la ambulancia
American estadounidense
amusement park el parque de atracciones
anemic anémico
anesthesia la anestesia
animal el animal
ankle el tobillo
antibiotic el antibiótico
antiques store la tienda de -antigüedades
antiseptic cream la crema antiséptica
anything algo
apartment el apartamento
appendix (body part) el apéndice
appetizer el aperitivo
appointment la cita
arcade el salón de juegos recreativos

area code el prefijo
arm el brazo
aromatherapy la aromaterapia
around (the corner) doblando (la esquina)
arrivals (airport) las llegadas
arrive v llegar
artery la arteria
arthritis la artritis
arts las letras
Asian asiático
aspirin la aspirina
asthmatic asmático
ATM el cajero automático
attack el asalto
attend v asistir
attraction (place) el sitio de interés
attractive guapo
Australia Australia
Australian australiano
automatic automático;
~ **car** coche automático
available disponible

B

baby el bebé; ~
bottle el biberón;
~ **wipe** la toallita;
~**sitter** el/la canguro
back la espalda;

~**ache** el dolor de espalda; ~**pack** la mochila
bag la maleta
baggage el equipaje;
~ **claim** la recogida de equipajes; ~
ticket el talón de equipaje
bakery la panadería
ballet el ballet
bandage la tirita
bank el banco
bar el bar
barbecue la barbacoa
barber la peluquería de caballeros
baseball el béisbol
basket (grocery store) la cesta
basketball el baloncesto
bathroom el baño
battery (car) la batería
battery la pila
battleground el campo de batalla
be v ser, estar
beach la playa
beautiful precioso
bed la cama; ~ **and breakfast** la pensión
begin v empezar
before antes de

beginner principiante
behind detrás de
beige beis
belt el cinturón
berth la litera
best el/la mejor
better mejor
bicycle la bicicleta
big grande
bigger más grande
bike route el sendero para bicicletas
bikini el biquini; ~ **wax** la depilación de las ingles
bill v (charge) cobrar; ~ n (money) el billete; ~ n (of sale) el recibo
bird el pájaro
birthday el cumpleaños
black negro
bladder la vejiga
bland soso
blanket la manta
bleed v sangrar
blood la sangre; ~ **pressure** la tensión arterial
blouse la blusa
blue azul
board v embarcar
boarding pass la tarjeta de embarque
boat el barco
bone el hueso
book el libro; ~**store** la librería
boots las botas
boring aburrido
botanical garden el jardín botánico
bother v molestar

bottle la botella; ~ **opener** el abrebotellas
bowl el cuenco
box la caja
boxing match la pelea de boxeo
boy el niño; ~**friend** el novio
bra el sujetador
bracelet la pulsera
brakes (car) los frenos
break v romper
break-in (burglary) el allanamiento de morada
breakdown la avería
breakfast el desayuno
breast el seno; ~**feed** dar el pecho
breathe v respirar
bridge el puente
briefs (clothing) los calzoncillos
bring v traer
British británico
broken roto
brooch el broche
broom la escoba
brother el hermano
brown marrón
bug el insecto
building el edificio
burn v (CD) grabar
bus el autobús; ~ **station** la estación de autobuses; ~ **stop** la parada de autobús; ~ **ticket** el billete de autobús; ~ **tour** el recorrido en autobús
business los negocios; ~ **card** la tarjeta de negocios; ~ **cent-**er el centro de negocios; ~ **class** la clase preferente; ~ **hours** el horario de atención al público
butcher el carnicero
buttocks las nalgas
buy v comprar
bye adiós

C

cabaret el cabaré
cabin (house) la cabaña; ~ **(ship)** el camarote
cable car el teleférico
cafe la cafetería
call v llamar; ~ n la llamada
calories las calorías
camera la cámara; **digital** ~ la cámara digital; ~ **case** la funda para la cámara; ~ **store** la tienda de fotografía
camp v acampar; ~ **stove** el hornillo; ~**site** el cámping
can opener el abrelatas
Canada Canadá
Canadian canadiense
cancel v cancelar
candy el caramelo
canned goods las conservas
canyon el cañón
car el coche; ~ **hire [BE]** el alquiler de coches; ~ **park [BE]** el aparcamiento; ~ **rental** el alquiler de coches; ~ **seat** el asiento de niño
carafe la garrafa
card la tarjeta; **ATM** ~ la tarjeta de cajero automático; **credit** ~ la tarjeta de crédito; **debit** ~ la tarjeta de débito; **phone** ~ la tarjeta telefónica
carry-on (piece of hand luggage) el equipaje de mano
cart (grocery store) el carrito; ~ **(luggage)** el carrito para el equipaje
carton el cartón; ~ **of cigarettes** el cartón de tabaco
case (amount) la caja
cash v cobrar; ~ n el efectivo; ~ **advance** sacar dinero de la tarjeta
cashier el cajero
casino el casino
castle el castillo
cathedral la catedral
cave la cueva
CD el CD
cell phone el teléfono móvil
Celsius el grado centígrado
centimeter el centímetro
certificate el certificado
chair la silla; ~ **lift** la telesilla
change v (buses) cambiar; ~ n (money) el cambio
charcoal el carbón

charge v (credit card) cobrar; ~ n (cost) el precio
cheap barato
cheaper más barato
check v (on something) revisar; ~ v (luggage) facturar; ~ n (payment) el cheque; ~-in (airport) la facturación; ~-in (hotel) el registro; ~-out (hotel) la salida
Cheers! ¡Salud!
chemical toilet el váter químico
chemist [BE] la farmacia
cheque [BE] el cheque
chest (body part) el pecho; ~ **pain** el dolor de pecho
chewing gum el chicle
child el niño; ~ **seat** la silla para niños
children's menu el menú para niños
children's portion la ración para niños
Chinese chino
chopsticks los palillos chinos
church la iglesia
cigar el puro
cigarette el cigarrillo
class la clase; **business** ~ la clase preferente; **economy** ~ la clase económica; **first** ~ la primera

clase
classical music la música clásica
clean v limpiar; ~ adj limpio; ~**ing product** el producto de limpieza; ~**ing supplies** los productos de limpieza
clear v (on an ATM) borrar
cliff el acantilado
cling film [BE] el film transparente
close v (a shop) cerrar
closed cerrado
clothing la ropa; ~ **store** la tienda de ropa
club la discoteca
coat el abrigo
coffee shop la cafetería
coin la moneda
colander el escurridor
cold n (sickness) el catarro; ~ adj (temperature) frío
colleague el compañero de trabajo
cologne la colonia
color el color
comb el peine
come v venir
complaint la queja
computer el ordenador
concert el concierto; ~ **hall** la sala de conciertos
condition (medical) el estado de salud
conditioner el suavizante

condom el preservativo
conference la conferencia
confirm v confirmar
congestion la congestión
connect v (internet) conectarse
connection (internet) la conexión; ~ (flight) la conexión de vuelo
constipated estreñido
consulate el consulado
consultant el consultor
contact v ponerse en contacto con
contact lens la lentilla de contacto; ~ **solution** el líquido de lentillas de contacto
contagious contagioso
convention hall el salón de congresos
conveyor belt la cinta transportadora
cook v cocinar
cooking gas el gas butano
cool (temperature) frío
copper el cobre
corkscrew el sacacorchos
cost v costar
cot el catre
cotton el algodón
cough v toser; ~ n la tos
country code el código de país
cover charge la entrada

crash v (car) estrellarse
cream (ointment) la pomada
credit card la tarjeta de crédito
crew neck el cuello redondo
crib la cuna
crystal el cristal
cup la taza
currency la moneda; ~ **exchange** el cambio de divisas; ~ **exchange office** la casa de cambio
current account [BE] la cuenta corriente
customs las aduanas
cut v (hair) cortar; ~ n (injury) el corte
cute mono
cycling el ciclismo

D

damage v causar daño
damaged ha sufrido daños
dance v bailar; ~ **club** la discoteca
dangerous peligroso
dark oscuro
date (calendar) la fecha
day el día
deaf sordo
debit card la tarjeta de débito
deck chair la tumbona
declare v declarar
decline v (credit card) rechazar
deeply hondo
degrees (temperature) los grados

delay v retrasarse
delete v (computer) borrar
delicatessen la charcutería
delicious delicioso
denim tela vaquero
dentist el dentista
denture la dentadura
deodorant el desodorante
department store los grandes almacenes
departures (airport) las salidas
deposit v depositar; ~ n (bank) el depósito bancario; ~ v (reserve a room) la fianza
desert el desierto
dessert el postre
detergent el detergente
develop v (film) revelar
diabetic diabético
dial v marcar
diamond el diamante
diaper el pañal
diarrhea la diarrea
diesel el diesel
difficult difícil
digital digital; ~ **camera** la cámara digital; ~ **photos** las fotos digitales; ~ **prints** las fotos digitales
dining room el comedor
dinner la cena
direction la dirección
dirty sucio
disabled discapacitado; ~ **accessible [BE]** el acceso para discapacitados
discharge (bodily fluid) la secreción
disconnect (computer) desconectar
discount el descuento
dish (kitchen) el plato; ~**washer** el lavavajillas; ~**washing liquid** el líquido lavavajillas
display v mostrar; ~ **case** la vitrina
disposable desechable; ~ **razor** la cuchilla desechable
dive v bucear
diving equipment el equipo de buceo
divorce v divorciar
dizzy mareado
doctor el médico
doll la muñeca
dollar (U.S.) el dólar
domestic nacional; ~ **flight** el vuelo nacional
door la puerta
dormitory el dormitorio
double bed la cama de matrimonio
downtown el centro
dozen la docena
drag lift el telesquí
dress (piece of clothing) el vestido; ~ **code** las normas de vestuario
drink v beber; ~ n la bebida; ~ **menu** la carta de bebidas; ~**ing water** el agua potable
drive v conducir
driver's license number el número de permiso de conducir
drop (medicine) la gota
drowsiness la somnolencia
dry cleaner la tintorería
dubbed doblada
during durante
duty (tax) el impuesto; ~**-free** libre de impuestos
DVD el DVD

E

ear la oreja; ~**ache** el dolor de oído
earlier más temprano
early temprano
earrings los pendientes
east el este
easy fácil
eat v comer
economy class la clase económica
elbow el codo
electric outlet el enchufe eléctrico
elevator el ascensor
e-mail v enviar un correo electrónico; ~ n el correo electrónico; ~ **address** la dirección de correo electrónico
emergency la emergencia; ~ **exit** la salida de urgencia
empty v vaciar
enamel (jewelry) el esmalte
end v terminar
English el inglés
engrave v grabar
enjoy v disfrutar
enter v entrar
entertainment el entretenimiento
entrance la entrada
envelope el sobre
equipment el equipo
escalators las escaleras mecánicas
e-ticket el billete electrónico
EU resident el/la residente de la UE
euro el euro
evening la noche
excess el exceso
exchange v (money) cambiar; ~ (goods) devolver; ~ n (place) la casa de cambio; ~ **rate** el tipo de cambio
excursion la excursión
excuse v (to get past) pedir perdón; ~ v (to get attention) disculparse
exhausted agotado
exit v salir; ~ n la salida
expensive caro
expert (skill level) experto
exposure (film) la foto
express rápido; ~

bus el autobús rápido; **~ train** el tren rápido
extension (phone) la extensión
extra adicional; **~ large** equis ele (XL)
extract v **(tooth)** extraer
eye el ojo
eyebrow wax la depilación de cejas

F

face la cara
facial la limpieza de cutis
family la familia
fan (appliance) el ventilador; **~ (souvenir)** el abanico
far lejos; **~-sighted** hipermétrope
farm la granja
fast rápido; **~ food** la comida rápida
faster más rápido
fat free sin grasa
father el padre
fax v enviar un fax; **~** n el fax; **~ number** el número de fax
fee la tasa
feed v alimentar
ferry el ferry
fever la fiebre
field (sports) el campo
fill v llenar; **~ out** v **(form)** rellenar
filling (tooth) el empaste
film (camera) el carrete

fine (fee for breaking law) la multa
finger el dedo; **~nail** la uña del dedo
fire fuego; **~ department** los bomberos; **~ door** la puerta de incendios
first primero; **~ class** la primera clase
fit (clothing) quedar bien
fitting room el probador
fix v **(repair)** reparar
flashlight la linterna
flight el vuelo
floor el suelo
flower la flor
folk music la música folk
food la comida
foot el pie
football [BE] el fútbol
for para/por
forecast el pronóstico
forest el bosque
fork el tenedor
form el formulario
formula (baby) la fórmula infantil
fort el fuerte
fountain la fuente
free gratuito
freezer el congelador
fresh fresco
friend el amigo
frying pan la sartén
full completo; **~-service** el servicio completo; **~-time** a

tiempo completo

G

game el partido
garage (parking) el garaje; **~ (repair)** el taller
garbage bag la bolsa de basura
gas la gasolina; **~ station** la gasolinera
gate (airport) la puerta
gay gay; **~ bar** el bar gay; **~ club** la discoteca gay
gel (hair) la gomina
get to v ir a
get off v **(a train/bus/ subway)** bajarse
gift el regalo; **~ shop** la tienda de regalos
girl la niña; **~friend** la novia
give v dar
glass (drinking) el vaso; **~ (material)** el vidrio
glasses las gafas
go v **(somewhere)** ir a
gold el oro
golf golf; **~ course** el campo de golf; **~ tournament** el torneo de golf
good n el producto; **~** adj bueno; **~ afternoon** buenas tardes; **~ evening** buenas noches; **~ morning** buenos días; **~bye** adiós

gram el gramo
grandchild el nieto
grandparent el abuelo
gray gris
green verde
grocery store el supermercado
ground la tierra; **~ floor** la planta baja; **~cloth** la tela impermeable
group el grupo
guide el guía; **~ book** la guía; **~ dog** el perro guía
gym el gimnasio
gynecologist el ginecólogo

H

hair el pelo; **~ dryer** el secador de pelo; **~ salon** la peluquería; **~brush** el cepillo de pelo; **~cut** el corte de pelo; **~spray** la laca; **~style** el peinado; **~stylist** el estilista
half medio; **~ hour** la media hora; **~-kilo** el medio kilo
hammer el martillo
hand la mano; **~ luggage [BE]** el equipaje de mano; **~bag [BE]** el bolso
handicapped discapacitado; **~-accessible** el acceso para discapacitados
hangover la resaca
happy feliz

hat el sombrero
have v tener
head (body part) la cabeza; **~ache** el dolor de cabeza; **~phones** los cascos
health la salud; **~ food store** la tienda de alimentos naturales
heart el corazón; **~ condition** padecer del corazón
heat v calentar; **~** n el calor
heater [heating BE] la calefacción
hello hola
helmet el casco
help v ayudar; **~** n la ayuda
here aquí
hi hola
high alto; **~chair** la trona; **~way** la autopista
hiking boots las botas de montaña
hill la colina
hire v [BE] alquilar; **~ car [BE]** el coche de alquiler
hitchhike v hacer autostop
hockey el hockey
holiday [BE] las vacaciones
horse track el hipódromo
hospital el hospital
hostel el albergue
hot (temperature) caliente;

~ (spicy) picante; **~ spring** el agua termale; **~ water** el agua caliente
hotel el hotel
hour la hora
house la casa; **~hold goods** los artículos para el hogar; **~keeping services** el servicio de limpieza de habitaciones
how (question) cómo; **~ much (question)** cuánto cuesta
hug v abrazar
hungry hambriento
hurt v **(have pain)** tener dolor
husband el marido

I

ibuprofen el ibuprofeno
ice el hielo; **~ hockey** el hockey sobre hielo
icy adj helado
identification el documento de identidad
ill v **(to feel)** encontrarse mal
in dentro
include v incluir
indoor pool la piscina cubierta
inexpensive barato
infected infectado
information (phone) el número de teléfono de información; **~ desk** el mostrador

de información
insect el insecto; **~ bite** la picadura de insecto; **~ repellent** el repelente de insectos
insert v introducir
insomnia el insomnio
instant message el mensaje instantáneo
insulin la insulina
insurance el seguro; **~ card** la tarjeta de seguro; **~ company** la compañía de seguros
interesting interesante
intermediate el nivel intermedio
international (airport area) internacional; **~ flight** el vuelo internacional; **~ student card** la tarjeta internacional de estudiante
internet la internet; **~ cafe** el cibercafé; **~ service** el servicio de internet; **wireless ~** el acceso inalámbrico
interpreter el/la intérprete
intersection el cruce
intestine el intestino
introduce v presentar
invoice [BE] la factura
Ireland Irlanda
Irish irlandés
iron v planchar; **~** n **(clothes)** la plancha
Italian italiano

J

jacket la chaqueta
jar el bote
jaw la mandíbula
jazz el jazz; **~ club** el club de jazz
jeans los vaqueros
jet ski la moto acuática
jeweler la joyería
jewelry las joyas
join v acompañar a
joint (body part) la articulación

K

key la llave; **~ card** la llave electrónica; **~ ring** el llavero
kiddie pool la piscina infantil
kidney (body part) el riñón
kilo el kilo; **~gram** el kilogramo; **~meter** el kilómetro
kiss v besar
kitchen la cocina; **~ foil [BE]** el papel de aluminio
knee la rodilla
knife el cuchillo

L

lace el encaje
lactose intolerant alérgico a la lactosa
lake el lago
large grande; **~r** más grande
last último
late (time) tarde; **~r** más tarde
launderette [BE] la

lavandería
laundromat la lavandería
laundry la colada; ~ **facility** la lavandería; ~ **service** el servicio de lavandería
lawyer el abogado
leather el cuero
to leave v salir
left (direction) la izquierda
leg la pierna
lens la lente
less menos
lesson la lección
letter la carta
library la biblioteca
life la vida; ~ **jacket** el chaleco salvavidas; ~**guard** el socorrista
lift n [BE] el ascensor; ~ v **(to give a ride)** llevar en coche; ~ **pass** el pase de acceso a los remontes
light n **(overhead)** la luz; ~ v **(cigarette)** dar fuego; ~**bulb** la bombilla
lighter el mechero
like v gustar; **I like** me gusta
line (train) la línea
linen el lino
lip el labio
liquor store la tienda de bebidas alcohólicas
liter el litro
little pequeño
live v vivir

liver (body part) el hígado
loafers los mocasines
local de la zona
lock v cerrar; ~ n el cerrojo
locker la taquilla
log on v **(computer)** iniciar sesión
log off v **(computer)** cerrar sesión
long largo; ~ **sleeves** las mangas largas; ~**sighted** [BE] hipermétrope
look v mirar
lose v **(something)** perder
lost perdido; ~ **and found** la oficina de objetos perdidos
lotion la crema hidratante
louder más alto
love v querer; ~ n el amor
low bajo; ~**er** más bajo
luggage el equipaje; ~ **cart** el carrito de equipaje; ~ **locker** la consigna automática; ~ **ticket** el talón de equipaje; **hand ~** [BE] el equipaje de mano
lunch la comida
lung el pulmón

M

magazine la revista
magnificent magnífico
mail v enviar por correo; ~ n el correo;

~**box** el buzón de correo
main principal; ~ **attractions** los principales sitios de interés; ~ **course** el plato principal
make up a prescription v [BE] despachar medicamentos
mall el centro comercial
man el hombre
manager el gerente
manicure la manicura
manual car el coche con transmisión manual
map el mapa
market el mercado
married casado
marry v casarse
mass (church service) la misa
massage el masaje
match la cerilla
meal la comida
measure v **(someone)** medir
measuring cup la taza medidora
measuring spoon la cuchara medidora
mechanic el mecánico
medicine el medicamento
medium (size) mediano
meet v **(someone)** conocer
meeting la reunión; ~ **room** la sala de

reuniones
membership card la tarjeta de socio
memorial (place) el monumento conmemorativo
memory card la tarjeta de memoria
mend v zurcir
menstrual cramps los dolores menstruales
menu la carta
message el mensaje
meter (parking) el parquímetro
microwave el microondas
midday [BE] el mediodía
midnight la medianoche
mileage el kilometraje
mini-bar el minibar
minute el minuto
missing desaparecido
mistake el error
mobile móvil; ~ **home** la caravana; ~ **phone** [BE] el teléfono móvil
mobility la movilidad
money el dinero
month el mes
mop la fregona
moped el ciclomotor
more más
morning la mañana
mosque la mezquita
mother la madre
motion sickness el mareo
motor el motor; ~ **boat** la lancha

motora; **~cycle** la motocicleta; **~way [BE]** la autopista

mountain la montaña; **~ bike** la bicicleta de montaña

mousse (hair) la espuma para el pelo

mouth *n* la boca

movie la película; **~ theater** el cine

mug *v* asaltar

muscle (body part) el músculo

museum el museo

music la música; **~ store** la tienda de música

N

nail la uña; **~ file** la lima de uñas; **~ salon** el salon de manicura

name el nombre

napkin la servilleta

nappy [BE] el pañale

nationality la nacionalidad

nature preserve la reserva natural

(be) nauseous *v* tener náuseas

near cerca; **~-sighted** miope; **~by** cerca de aquí

neck el cuello

necklace el collar

need *v* necesitar

newspaper el periódico

newsstand el quiosco

next próximo

nice *adj* amable

night la noche; **~club** la discoteca

no no

non sin; **~-alcoholic** sin alcohol; **~-smoking** para no fumadores

noon el mediodía

north el norte

nose la nariz

note [BE] el billete

nothing nada

notify *v* avisar

novice (skill level) principiante

now ahora

number el número

nurse el enfermero/la enfermera

O

office la oficina; **~ hours (doctor's)** las horas de consulta; **~ hours (other offices)** el horario de oficina

off-licence [BE] la tienda de bebidas alcohólicas

oil el aceite

OK de acuerdo

old *adj* viejo

on the corner en la esquina

once una vez

one uno; **~-way ticket** el billete de ida; **~-way street** la calle de sentido único

only solamente

open *v* abrir; **~** *adj* abierto

opera la ópera; **~ house** el teatro de la ópera

opposite frente a

optician el oculista

orange (color) naranja

orchestra la orquesta

order *v* pedir

outdoor pool la piscina exterior

outside fuera

over sobre; **~ the counter (medication)** sin receta; **~look (scenic place)** el mirador; **~night** por la noche

oxygen treatment la oxigenoterapia

P

p.m. de la tarde

pacifier el chupete

pack *v* hacer las maletas

package el paquete

paddling pool [BE] la piscina infantil

pad [BE] la compresa

pain el dolor

pajamas los pijamas

palace el palacio

pants los pantalones

pantyhose las medias

paper el papel; **~ towel** el papel de cocina

paracetamol [BE] el paracetamol

park *v* aparcar; **~** *n* el parque; **~ing garage** el párking; **~ing lot** el

aparcamiento

parliament building el palacio de las cortes

part (for car) la pieza; **~-time** a tiempo parcial

pass through *v* estar de paso

passenger el pasajero

passport el pasaporte; **~ control** el control de pasaportes

password la contraseña

pastry shop la pastelería

path el camino

pay *v* pagar; **~ phone** el teléfono público

peak (of a mountain) la cima

pearl la perla

pedestrian el peatón

pediatrician el pediatra

pedicure la pedicura

pen el bolígrafo

penicillin la penicilina

penis el pene

per por; **~ day** por día; **~ hour** por hora; **~ night** por noche; **~ week** por semana

perfume el perfume

period (menstrual) la regla; **~ (of time)** la época

permit *v* permitir

petite las tallas pequeñas

petrol la gasolina; **~**

station la gaso-
lina
pewter el peltre
pharmacy la farmacia
phone v
hacer una llamada;
~ n el teléfono; ~
call la llamada de
teléfono; ~ **card** la
tarjeta telefónica; ~
number el número
de teléfono
photo la foto;
~**copy** la fotocopia;
~**graphy** la foto-
grafía
pick up v (some-
thing) recoger
picnic area la zona
para picnic
piece el trozo
Pill (birth control) la
píldora
pillow la almohada
**personal identifica-
tion number
(PIN)** la clave
pink rosa
piste [BE] la pista; ~
map [BE] el mapa
de pistas
pizzeria la pizzería
place v (a bet) hacer
una apuesta
plane el avión
plastic wrap el film
transparente
plate el plato
**platform [BE]
(train)** el andén
platinum el platino
play v jugar; ~ n
(theater) la obra de
teatro; ~**ground** el

patio de recreo;
~**pen** el parque
please por favor
pleasure el placer
plunger el desa-
tascador
plus size la talla
grande
pocket el bolsillo
poison el veneno
poles (skiing) los
bastones
police la policía; ~
report el certificado
de la policía; ~ **sta-
tion** la comisaría
pond el estanque
pool la piscina
pop music la música
pop
portion la ración
post [BE] el correo;
~ **office** la oficina
de correos; ~**box
[BE]** el buzón de
correos; ~**card** la
tarjeta postal
pot la olla
pottery la cerámica
**pounds (British
sterling)** las libras
esterlinas
pregnant embarazada
prescribe v recetar
prescription la receta
press v (cloth-
ing) planchar
price el precio
print v imprimir
problem el problema
produce las frutas y
verduras; ~ **store** la
frutería y verdulería
prohibit v prohibir

pronounce v
pronunciar
public el público
pull v (door sign) tirar
purple morado
purse el bolso
push v (door
sign) empujar;
~**chair [BE]** el
cochecito de niño

Q

quality n la calidad
question la pregunta
quiet adj tranquilo

R

racetrack el circuito
de carreras
racket (sports) la
raqueta
**railway station
[BE]** la estación de
trenes
rain la lluvia;
~**coat** el chubas-
quero; ~**forest** el
bosque pluvial;
~**y** adv lluvioso
rap (music) el rap
rape v violar; ~ n la
violación
rash la erupción
cutánea
razor blade la hoja de
afeitar
reach v localizar
ready listo
real auténtico
receipt el recibo
receive v recibir
reception la recepción
recharge v recargar
recommend v

recomendar
recommendation la
recomendación
recycle v reciclar
red rojo
refrigerator n la
nevera
region la región
registered mail el
correo certificado
regular normal
relationship la
relación
rent v alquilar
rental car el coche de
alquiler
repair v arreglar
repeat v repetir
reservation la reserva;
~ **desk** la taquilla
reserve v reservar
restaurant el
restaurante
restroom el servicio
retired jubilado
return v (some-
thing) devolver; ~ n
[BE] la ida y vuelta
rib (body part) la
costilla
right (direction) derecha; ~ **of way** prior-
idad de paso
ring el anillo
river n el río
road map el mapa de
carreteras
rob v atracar
robbed atracado
romantic romántico
room la habitación;
~ **key** la llave de
habitación; ~ **ser-
vice** el servicio de

habitaciones
round-trip ida y vuelta
route la ruta
rowboat la barca de remos
rubbish [BE] la basura; ~ **bag [BE]** la bolsa de basura
rugby el rugby
ruins las ruinas
rush la prisa

S

sad triste
safe *n* la caja fuerte; ~ *adj* seguro
sales tax el IVA
same mismo
sandals las sandalias
sanitary napkin la compresa
saucepan el cazo
sauna la sauna
save *v* (**computer**) guardar
savings (account) la cuenta de ahorro
scanner el escáner
scarf la bufanda
schedule *v* programar; ~ *n* el horario
school el colegio
science la ciencia
scissors las tijeras
sea el mar
seat el asiento
security la seguridad
see *v* ver
self-service el autoservicio
sell *v* vender
seminar el seminario
send *v* enviar
senior citizen jubilado

separated (marriage) -separado
serious serio
service (in a restaurant) el servicio
sexually transmitted disease (STD) la enfermedad de transmisión sexual
shampoo el champú
sharp afilado
shaving cream la crema de afeitar
sheet la sábana
ship *v* enviar
shirt la camisa
shoe store la zapatería
shoes los zapatos
shop *v* comprar
shopping ir de compras; ~ **area** la zona de compras; ~ **centre [BE]** el centro comercial; ~ **mall** el centro comercial
short corto; ~ **sleeves** las mangas cortas; ~**s** los pantalones cortos; ~**-sighted [BE]** miope
shoulder el hombro
show *v* enseñar
shower la ducha
shrine el santuario
sick enfermo
side el lado; ~ **dish** la guarnición; ~ **effect** el efecto secundario; ~ **order** la guarnición
sightsee *v* hacer turismo
sightseeing tour el

recorrido turístico
sign *v* (**name**) firmar
silk la seda
silver la plata
single (unmarried) soltero; ~ **bed** la cama; ~ **prints** una copia; ~ **room** una habitación individual
sink el lavabo
sister la hermana
sit *v* sentarse
size la talla
skin la piel
skirt la falda
ski *v* esquiar; ~ *n* el esquí; ~ **lift** el telesquí
sleep *v* dormir; ~**er car** el coche cama; ~**ing bag** el saco de dormir
slice *v* cortar en rodajas
slippers las zapatillas
slower más despacio
slowly despacio
small pequeño
smaller más pequeño
smoke *v* fumar
smoking (area) la zona de fumadores
snack bar la cafetería
sneakers las zapatillas de deporte
snorkeling equipment el equipo de esnórquel
snow la nieve; ~**board** la tabla de snowboard; ~**shoe** la raqueta de nieve; ~**y** nevado

soap el jabón
soccer el fútbol
sock el calcetín
some alguno
soother [BE] el chupete
sore throat las anginas
sorry lo siento
south el sur
souvenir el recuerdo; ~ **store** la tienda de recuerdos
spa el centro de salud y belleza
Spain España
Spanish el español
spatula la espátula
speak *v* hablar
special (food) la especialidad de la casa
specialist (doctor) el especialista
specimen el ejemplar
speeding el exceso de velocidad
spell *v* deletrear
spicy picante
spine (body part) la columna vertebral
spoon la cuchara
sports los deportes; ~ **massage** el masaje deportivo
sporting goods store la tienda de deportes
sprain el esguince
square cuadrado; ~ **kilometer** el kilómetro cuadrado; ~ **meter** el metro cuadrado

stadium el estadio

stairs las escaleras

stamp v (a ticket) picar; ~ n (postage) el sello

start v empezar

starter [BE] el aperitivo

station la estación; **bus ~** la estación de autobuses; **gas ~** la gasolinera; **muster ~** [BE] el punto de reunión; **petrol ~** [BE] la gasolinera; **subway ~** el metro; **train ~** la estación de tren

statue la estatua

stay v quedarse

steal v robar

steep empinado

sterling silver la plata esterlina

sting el escozor

stolen robado

stomach el estómago; **~ache** el dolor de estómago

stop v pararse; ~ n la parada

storey [BE] la planta

stove el horno

straight recto

strange extraño

stream el arroyo

stroller el cochecito

student el estudiante

study v estudiar

stunning impresionante

subtitle el subtítulo

subway el metro; ~

station la estación de metro

suit el traje

suitcase la maleta

sun el sol; **~block** el protector solar total; **~burn** la quemadura solar; **~glasses** las gafas de sol; **~ny** soleado; **~screen** el protector solar; **~stroke** la insolación

super (fuel) súper; **~market** el supermercado

surfboard la tabla de surf

surgical spirit [BE] el alcohol etílico

swallow v tragar

sweater el jersey

sweatshirt la sudadera

sweet (taste) dulce; **~s** [BE] los caramelos

swelling la hinchazón

swim v nadar; **~suit** el bañador

symbol (keyboard) el símbolo

synagogue la sinagoga

T

table la mesa

tablet (medicine) el comprimido

take v llevar; **~ away** [BE] para llevar

tampon el tampón

tapas bar el bar de tapas

taste v probar

taxi el taxi

team el equipo

telephone el teléfono

temporary provisional

tennis el tenis

tent la tienda de campaña; **~ peg** la estaca; **~ pole** el mástil

terminal (airport) la terminal

terracotta la terracotta

terrible terrible

text v (send a message) enviar un mensaje de texto; **~ n (message)** el texto

thank v dar las gracias a; **~ you** gracias

that eso

theater el teatro

there ahí

thief el ladrón

thigh el muslo

thirsty sediento

this esto

throat la garganta

ticket el billete; **~ office** el despacho de billetes; **~ed passenger** el pasajero con billete

tie (clothing) la corbata

time el tiempo; **~table** [BE] el horario

tire la rueda

tired cansado

tissue el pañuelo de paper

tobacconist el estanco

today hoy

toe el dedo del pie; **~nail** la uña del pie

toilet [BE] el servicio; **~ paper** el papel higiénico

tomorrow mañana

tongue la lengua

tonight esta noche

too demasiado

tooth el diente; **~brush** el cepillo de dientes; **~paste** la pasta de dientes

total (amount) el total

tough (food) duro

tourist el turista; **~ information office** la oficina de turismo

tour el recorrido turístico

tow truck la grúa

towel la toalla

tower la torre

town la ciudad; **~ hall** el ayuntamiento; **~ map** el mapa de ciudad; **~ square** la plaza

toy el juguete; **~ store** la tienda de juguetes

track (train) el andén

traditional tradicional

traffic light el semáforo

trail la pista; **~ map** el mapa de la pista

trailer el remolque

train el tren; **~ station** la estación

de tren
transfer *v* cambiar
translate *v* traducir
trash la basura
travel *v* viajar; **~ agency** la agencia de viajes; **~ sickness** el mareo; **~er's check [cheque BE]** el cheque de viaje
tree el árbol
trim (hair cut) cortarse las puntas
trip el viaje
trolley [BE] el carrito
trousers [BE] los pantalones
T-shirt la camiseta
turn off *v* apagar
turn on *v* encender
TV la televisión
type *v* escribir a máquina
tyre [BE] la rueda

U

United Kingdom (U.K.) el Reino Unido
United States (U.S.) los Estados Unidos
ugly feo
umbrella el paraguas
unattended desatendido
unconscious inconsciente
underground [BE] el metro; **~ station [BE]** la estación de metro
underpants [BE] los

calzoncillos
understand *v* entender
underwear la ropa interior
university la universidad
unleaded (gas) la gasolina sin plomo
upper superior
urgent urgente
use *v* usar
username el nombre de usuario
utensil el cubierto

V

vacancy la habitación libre
vacation las vacaciones
vaccination la vacuna
vacuum cleaner la aspiradora
vaginal infection la infección vaginal
valid validez
valley el valle
valuable valioso
VAT [BE] el IVA
vegetarian vegetariano
vehicle registration el registro del coche
viewpoint [BE] el mirador
village el pueblo
vineyard la viña
visa (passport document) el visado
visit *v* visitar; **~ing hours** el horario de visita
visually impaired la

persona con discapacidad visual
vitamin la vitamina
V-neck el cuello de pico
vomit *v* vomitar

W

wait *v* esperar; **~** *n* la espera; **~ing room** la sala de espera
waiter el camarero
waitress la camarera
wake *v* despertarse; **~-up call** la llamada despertador
walk *v* caminar; **~** *n* la caminata; **~ing route** la ruta de senderismo
wallet la cartera
warm *v* (something) calentar; **~** *adj* (temperature) calor
washing machine la lavadora
watch el reloj
waterfall la cascada
weather el tiempo
week la semana; **~end** el fin de semana; **~ly** semanal
welcome *v* acoger
well bien; **~-rested** descansado
west el oeste
what (question) qué
wheelchair la silla de ruedas; **~ ramp** la rampa para silla de ruedas
when (ques-

tion) cuándo
where (question) dónde
white blanco; **~ gold** el oro blanco
who (question) quién
widowed viudo
wife la mujer
window la ventana; **~ case** el escaparate
windsurfer el surfista
wine list la carta de vinos
wireless inalámbrico; **~ internet** el acceso inalámbrico a internet; **~ internet service** el servicio inalámbrico a internet; **~ phone** el teléfono móvil
with con
withdraw *v* retirar; **~al (bank)** retirar fondos
without sin
woman la mujer
wool la lana
work *v* trabajar
wrap *v* envolver
wrist la muñeca
write *v* escribir

Y

year el año
yellow amarillo
yes sí
yesterday ayer
young joven
youth hostel el albergue juvenil

Z

zoo el zoológico

SPANISH–ENGLISH

A

a tiempo completo full-time
a tiempo parcial part-time
la abadía abbey
el abanico fan (souvenir)
abierto *adj* open
el abogado lawyer
abrazar *v* hug
el abrebotellas bottle opener
el abrelatas can opener
el abrigo coat
abrir *v* open
el abuelo grandparent
aburrido boring
acampar *v* camp
el acantilado cliff
el acceso access; ~ inalámbrico a internet wireless internet; ~ para discapacitados handicapped- [disabled-BE] accessible
el accidente accident
el aceite oil
aceptar *v* accept
acoger *v* welcome
acompañar a *v* join
la acupuntura acupuncture
el adaptador adapter
adicional extra
adiós goodbye
las aduanas customs
el aeropuerto airport

afilado sharp
la agencia agency; ~ de viajes travel agency
agotado exhausted
el agua water; ~ caliente hot water; ~ potable drinking water
las aguas termales hot spring
ahí there
ahora now
el aire air, air pump; ~ acondicionado air conditioning
el albergue hostel; ~ juvenil youth hostel
alérgico allergic; ~ a la lactosa lactose intolerant
algo anything
el algodón cotton
alguno some
alimentar *v* feed
el allanamiento de morada break-in (burglary)
la almohada pillow
el alojamiento accommodation
alquilar *v* rent [hire BE]; el ~ de coches car rental [hire BE]
alto high
amable nice
amarillo yellow
la ambulancia am-

bulance
el amigo friend
el amor *n* love
el andén track [platform BE] (train)
anémico anemic
la anestesia anesthesia
las anginas sore throat
el anillo ring
el animal animal
antes de before
el antibiótico antibiotic
el año year
apagar *v* turn off
el aparcamiento parking lot [car park BE]
aparcar *v* park
el apartamento apartment
el apéndice appendix (body part)
el aperitivo appetizer [starter BE]
aquí here
el árbol tree
la aromaterapia aromatherapy
arreglar *v* repair
el arroyo stream
la arteria artery
la articulación joint (body part)
los artículos goods; ~ para el hogar household good
la artritis arthritis

asaltar *v* mug
el asalto attack
el ascensor elevator [lift BE]
asiático Asian
el asiento seat; ~ de niño car seat; ~ de pasillo aisle seat
asistir *v* attend
asmático asthmatic
la aspiradora vacuum cleaner
la aspirina aspirin
atracado robbed
atracar *v* rob
Australia Australia
australiano Australian
auténtico real
el autobús bus; ~ rápido express bus
automático automatic
la autopista highway [motorway BE]
el autoservicio self-service
la avería breakdown
el avión airplane, plane
avisar *v* notify
ayer yesterday
la ayuda *n* help
ayudar *v* help
el ayuntamiento town hall
azul blue

B

bailar *v* dance
bajarse *v* get off (a train, bus, subway)

bajo low
el ballet ballet
el baloncesto basketball
el bálsamo para después del afeitado aftershave
el banco bank
el bañador swimsuit
el baño bathroom
el bar bar; **~ de tapas** tapas bar; **~ gay** gay bar
barato cheap, inexpensive
la barbacoa barbecue
la barca de remos rowboat
el barco boat
los bastones poles (skiing)
la basura trash [rubbish BE]
la batería battery (car)
el bebé baby
beber v drink
la bebida n drink
beis beige
el béisbol baseball
besar v kiss
el biberón baby bottle
la biblioteca library
la bicicleta bicycle; **~ de montaña** mountain bike
el billete n bill (money); **~** ticket; **~ de autobús** bus ticket; **~ de ida** one-way (ticket); **~ de ida y vuelta** round trip [return BE]; **~ electrónico** e-ticket

el biquini bikini
blanco white
la blusa blouse
la boca mouth
el bolígrafo pen
la bolsa de basura garbage [rubbish BE] bag
el bolsillo pocket
el bolso purse [handbag BE]
los bomberos fire department
la bombilla lightbulb
borrar v clear (on an ATM); **~** v delete (computer)
el bosque forest; **~ pluvial** rainforest
las botas boots; **~ de montaña** hiking boots
el bote jar
la botella bottle
el brazo arm
británico British
el broche brooch
bucear to dive
bueno adj good
buenas noches good evening
buenas tardes good afternoon
buenos días good morning
la bufanda scarf
el buzón de correo mailbox [postbox BE]

C

la cabaña cabin (house)
el cabaré cabaret

la cabeza head (body part)
la cafetería cafe, coffee shop, snack bar
la caja case (amount); **~ fuerte** n safe
el cajero cashier; **~ automático** ATM
el calcetín sock
la calefacción heater [heating BE]
calentar v heat, warm
la calidad quality
la calle de sentido único one-way street
calor hot, warm (temperature)
las calorías calories
los calzoncillos briefs [underpants BE] (clothing)
la cama single bed; **~ de matrimonio** double bed
la cámara camera; **~ digital** digital camera
la camarera waitress
el camarero waiter
el camarote cabin (ship)
cambiar v change, exchange, transfer
el cambio n change (money); **~ de divisas** currency exchange
caminar v walk
la caminata n walk
el camino path
la camisa shirt
la camiseta T-shirt
el cámping campsite

el campo field (sports); **~ de batalla** battleground; **~ de golf** golf course
Canadá Canada
canadiense Canadian
cancelar v cancel
el/la canguro babysitter
cansado tired
el cañón canyon
la cara face
los caramelos candy [sweets BE]
la caravana mobile home
el carbón charcoal
el carnicero butcher
caro expensive
el carrete film (camera)
el carrito cart [trolley BE] (grocery store); **~ de equipaje** luggage cart
la carta letter
la carta n menu; **~ de bebidas** drink menu; **~ para niños** children's menu; **~ de vinos** wine list
la cartera n wallet
el cartón carton; **~ de tabaco** carton of cigarettes
la casa house; **~ de cambio** currency exchange office
casado married
casarse v marry
la cascada waterfall
el casco helmet

los cascos headphones
el casino casino
el castillo castle
el catarro cold (sickness)
la catedral cathedral
el catre cot
causar daño *v* damage
el cazo saucepan
el CD CD
la cena dinner
el centímetro centimeter
el centro downtown area; **~ comercial** shopping mall [centre BE]; **~ de negocios** business center; **~ de salud y belleza** spa
el cepillo de pelo hair brush
la cerámica pottery
cerca near; **~ de aquí** nearby
la cerilla *n* match
cerrado closed
cerrar *v* close, lock; **~ sesión** *v* log off (computer)
el cerrojo *n* lock
el certificado certificate; **~ de la policía** police report
la cesta basket (grocery store)
el chaleco salvavidas life jacket
el champú shampoo
la chaqueta jacket
la charcutería delicatessen

el cheque *n* check [cheque BE] (payment); **~ de viaje** traveler's check [cheque BE]
el chicle chewing gum
chino Chinese
el chubasquero raincoat
el chupete pacifier [soother BE]
el cibercafé internet cafe
el ciclismo cycling
el ciclomotor moped
la ciencia science
el cigarrillo cigarette
la cima peak (of a mountain)
el cine movie theater
la cinta transportadora conveyor belt
el cinturón *n* belt
el circuito de carreras racetrack
la cita appointment
la ciudad town
la clase class; **~ económica** economy class; **~ preferente** business class
la clave personal identification number (PIN)
el club de jazz jazz club
cobrar *v* bill (charge); **~** *v* cash; **~** *v* charge (credit card)
el cobre copper
el coche *n* car; **~ de alquiler** rental [hire BE] car; **~ automático** automatic car; **~ cama** sleeper [sleeping BE] car; **~ con transmisión manual** manual car
el cochecito stroller [pushchair BE]
la cocina kitchen
cocinar *v* cook
el código de país country code
el codo elbow
la colada laundry
el colegio school
la colina hill
el collar necklace
la colonia cologne
el color color
la columna vertebral spine (body part)
el comedor dining room
comer *v* eat
la comida food, lunch, meal; **~ rápida** fast food
la comisaría police station
cómo how
el compañero de trabajo colleague
la compañía company; **~ aérea** airline; **~ de seguros** insurance company
comprar *v* buy, shop
la compresa sanitary napkin [pad BE]
el comprimido tablet (medicine)
con with; **~ plomo** leaded (gas)
el concierto concert

conducir *v* drive
conectarse *v* connect (internet)
la conexión connection (internet); **~ de vuelo** connection (flight)
la conferencia conference
confirmar *v* confirm
el congelador freezer
la congestión congestion
conocer *v* meet (someone)
la consigna automática luggage locker
el consulado Consulate
el consultor consultant
contagioso contagious
la contraseña password
el control de pasaportes passport control
el corazón heart
la corbata tie (clothing)
el correo *n* mail [post BE]; **~ aéreo** airmail; **~ certificado** registered mail; **~ electrónico** *n* e-mail
cortar *v* cut (hair); **~ en rodajas** to slice
cortarse las puntas *v* trim (hair cut)
el corte *n* cut (injury); **~ de pelo** haircut
corto short

costar v cost

la costilla rib (body part)

la crema cream; **~ antiséptica** antiseptic cream; **~ de afeitar** shaving cream; **~ hidratante** lotion

el cristal crystal

el cruce intersection

cuándo when (question)

cuánto cuesta how much

el cubierto utensil

la cuchara spoon; **~ medidora** measuring spoon

la cucharadita teaspoon

la cuchilla desechable disposable razor

el cuchillo knife

el cuello neck; **~ de pico** V-neck; **~ redondo** crew neck

el cuenco bowl

la cuenta account; **~ de ahorro** savings account; **~ corriente** checking [current BE] account

cuero leather

la cueva cave

el cumpleaños birthday

la cuna crib

D

dar to give; **~ el pecho** breastfeed; **~ fuego** light (ciga-

rette); **~ las gracias a** v thank

de from, of; **~ acuerdo** OK; **~ la mañana** a.m.; **~ la tarde** p.m.; **~ la zona** local

declarar v declare

el dedo finger; **~ del pie** toe

deletrear v spell

delicioso delicious

la dentadura denture

el dentista dentist

dentro in

la depilacion wax; **~ de cejas** eyebrow wax; **~ de las ingles** bikini wax

deportes sports

depositar v deposit

el depósito bancario deposit (bank)

la derecha right (direction)

desaparecido missing

el desatascador plunger

desatendido unattended

el desayuno breakfast

descansado well-rested

desconectar v disconnect (computer)

el descuento discount

desechable disposable

el desierto desert

el desodorante deodorant

despachar medicamentos v fill [make up BE] a prescription

el despacho de billetes ticket office

despacio slowly

despertarse v wake

después after

el detergente detergent

detrás de behind (direction)

devolver v exchange, return (goods)

el día day

diabético diabetic

el diamante diamond

la diarrea diarrhea

el diente tooth

el diesel diesel

difícil difficult

digital digital

el dinero money

la dirección direction

la dirección address; **~ de correo electrónico** e-mail address

discapacitado handicapped [disabled BE]

la discoteca club (dance, night); **~ gay** gay club

disculparse v excuse (to get attention)

disfrutar v enjoy

disponible available

divorciar v divorce

doblada dubbed

doblando (la esquina) around (the corner)

la docena dozen

el documento de identidad identification

el dólar dollar (U.S.)

el dolor pain; **~ de cabeza** headache; **~ de espalda** backache; **~ de estómago** stomachache; **~ de oído** earache; **~ de pecho** chest pain

los dolores menstruales menstrual cramps

dónde where (question)

dormir v sleep

el dormitorio dormitory

la ducha shower

dulce sweet (taste)

durante during

el DVD DVD

E

la edad age

el edificio building

el efectivo cash

el efecto secundario side effect

el ejemplar specimen

embarazada pregnant

embarcar v board

la emergencia emergency

el empaste filling (tooth)

empezar v begin, start

empinado steep

empujar v push (door sign)

en la esquina on the corner

el encaje lace

encender v turn on

el enchufe eléctrico electric outlet

encontrarse mal *v*
be ill
**la enfermedad
de transmisión
sexual** sexually
transmitted disease
(STD)
**el enfermero/la
enfermera** nurse
enfermo sick
enseñar *v* show
entender *v* under-
stand
la entrada admission/
cover charge; **~**
entrance
entrar *v* enter
**el entretenimien-
to** entertainment
enviar *v* send, ship;
~ por correo *v*
mail; **~ un correo
electrónico** *v*
e-mail; **~ un fax** *v*
fax; **~ un mensaje
de texto** *v* text (send
a message)
envolver *v* wrap
la época period (of
time)
el equipaje luggage
(baggage BE); **~ de
mano** carry-on
(piece of hand
luggage)
el equipo team
el equipo equipment;
~ de buceo diving
equipment; **~ de
esnórquel** snorkel-
ing equipment
equis ele (XL) extra
large
el error mistake

**la erupción
cutánea** rash
las escaleras stairs;
~ mecánicas es-
calators
el escáner scanner
el escaparate window
case
la escoba broom
el escozor sting
escribir *v* write; **~ a
máquina** *v* type
el escurridor colander
el esguince sprain
el esmalte enamel
(jewelry)
eso that
la espalda back
España Spain
el español Spanish
la espátula spatula
**la especialidad de la
casa** special (food)
el especialista spe-
cialist (doctor)
la espera *n* wait
esperar *v* wait
**la espuma para el
pelo** mousse (hair)
el esquí *n* ski
esquiar *v* ski
**los esquís acuáti-
cos** water skis
esta noche tonight
la estaca tent peg
la estación sta-
tion; **~ de auto-
buses** bus station;
~ de metro subway
(underground BE) sta-
tion; **~ de tren** train
(railway BE) station
el estadio stadium
el estado de

salud condition
(medical)
**los Estados Uni-
dos** United States
(U.S.)
**estadoun-
idense** American
el estanco tobacconist
el estanque pond
estar *v* be; **~ de
paso** *v* pass through
la estatua statue
el este east
el estilista hairstylist
esto this
el estómago stomach
estrellarse *v* crash
(car)
estreñido constipated
estudiando studying
el estudiante student
estudiar *v* study
el euro euro
el exceso excess;
~ de velocidad
speeding
la excursión excursion
experto expert (skill
level)
la extensión extension
(phone)
extraer *v* extract
(tooth)
extraño strange

F

fácil *adj* easy
la factura bill (invoice
BE)
la facturación check-
in (airport)
facturar check
(luggage)
la falda skirt

la familia family
la farmacia pharmacy
(chemist BE)
el fax *n* fax
la fecha date
(calendar)
feliz *adj* happy
feo *adj* ugly
el ferry ferry
la fianza deposit (to
reserve a room)
la fiebre fever
**el film transpar-
ente** plastic wrap
(cling film BE)
**el fin de se-
mana** weekend
firmar *v* sign (name)
la flor flower
**la fórmula infan-
til** formula (baby)
el formulario form
la foto exposure
(film); **~ photo**;
~copia photocopy;
~grafía photogra-
phy; **~ digital** digital
photo
la fregona mop
los frenos brakes (car)
frente a opposite
fresco fresh
frío *adj* cold (tem-
perature)
**las frutas y ver-
duras** produce
**la frutería y verdul-
ería** produce store
el fuego fire
la fuente fountain
fuera outside
el fuerte fort
fumar *v* smoke
la funda para la cá-

mara camera case

el fútbol soccer [football BE]

G

las gafas glasses; **~ de sol** sunglasses

el garaje garage (parking)

la garganta throat

la garrafa carafe

el gas butano cooking gas

la gasolina gas [petrol BE]; **~ sin plomo** unleaded gas

la gasolinera gas [petrol BE] station

gay gay

el gerente manager

el gimnasio gym

el ginecólogo gynecologist

la gomina gel (hair)

la gota drop (medicine)

grabar v burn (CD); **~** v engrave

gracias thank you

los grados degrees (temperature); **~ centígrado** Celsius

el gramo gram

grande large

los grandes almacenes department store

la granja farm

gratuito free

gris gray

la grúa tow truck

el grupo group

guapo attractive

guardar v save

(computer)

la guarnición side dish, order

el guía guide

la guía guide book; **~ de tiendas** store directory

gustar v like; **me gusta** I like

H

ha sufrido daños damaged

la habitación room; **~ individual** single room; **~ libre** vacancy

hablar v speak

hacer v have; **~ una apuesta** v place (a bet); **~ un arreglo** v alter; **~ una llamada** v phone; **~ las maletas** v pack; **~ turismo** sightseeing

hambriento hungry

helado icy

la hermana sister

el hermano brother

el hielo ice

el hígado liver (body part)

la hinchazón swelling

hipermétrope far-sighted [long-sighted BE]

el hipódromo horse-track

el hockey hockey; **~ sobre hielo** ice hockey

la hoja de afeitar razor blade

hola hello

el hombre man

el hombro shoulder

hondo deeply

la hora hour

el horario n schedule [timetable BE]

los horarios hours; **~ de atención al público** business hours; **~ de oficina** office hours; **~ de visita** visiting hours

las horas de consulta office hours (doctor's)

el hornillo camp stove

el horno stove

el hospital hospital

el hotel hotel

hoy today

el hueso bone

I

el ibuprofeno ibuprofen

la ida y vuelta round-trip [return BE]

la iglesia church

impresionante stunning

imprimir v print

el impuesto duty (tax)

incluir v include

inconsciente unconscious

increíble amazing

la infección vaginal vaginal infection

infectado infected

el inglés English

iniciar sesión v log on

(computer)

el insecto bug

la insolación sun-stroke

el insomnio insomnia

la insulina insulin

interesante interesting

internacional international (airport area)

la internet internet

el/la intérprete interpreter

el intestino intestine

introducir v insert

ir a v go (somewhere)

ir de compras v go shopping

Irlanda Ireland

irlandés Irish

el IVA sales tax [VAT BE]

la izquierda left (direction)

J

el jabón soap

el jardín botánico botanical garden

el jazz jazz

el jersey sweater

joven young

las joyas jewelry

la joyería jeweler

jubilado retired

jugar v play

el juguete toy

K

el kilo kilo; **~gramo** kilogram; **~metraje** mileage

el kilómetro kilometer; **~ cuadra-do** square kilometer

L

el labio lip
la laca hairspray
el ladrón thief
el lago lake
la lana wool
la lancha motora motor boat
largo long
el lavabo sink
la lavadora washing machine
la lavandería laundromat [launderette BE]
lavar v wash
el lavavajillas dishwasher
la lección lesson
lejos far
la lengua tongue
la lente lens
las lentillas de contacto contact lens
las letras arts
las libras esterlinas pounds (British sterling)
libre de impuestos duty-free
la librería bookstore
el libro book
la lima de uñas nail file
limpiar v clean
la limpieza de cutis facial
limpio adj clean
la línea line (train)
el lino linen
la linterna flashlight

el líquido liquid; **~ de lentillas de contacto** contact lens solution; **~ lavavajillas** dish-washing liquid
listo ready
la litera berth
el litro liter
la llamada n call; **~ de teléfono** phone call; **~ despertador** wake-up call
llamar v call
la llave key; **~ de habitación** room key; **~ electrónica** key card
el llavero key ring
las llegadas arrivals (airport)
llegar v arrive
llenar v fill
llevar v take; **~ en coche** lift (to give a ride)
la lluvia rain
lluvioso rainy
lo siento sorry
localizar v reach
la luz light (overhead)

M

la madre mother
magnífico magnificent
el malestar estomacal upset stomach
la maleta bag, suitcase
la mandíbula jaw
las mangas cortas short sleeves
las mangas lar-

gas long sleeves
la manicura manicure
la mano hand
la manta blanket
mañana tomorrow; **la ~** morning
el mapa map; **~ de carreteras** road map; **~ de ciudad** town map; **~ la pista** trail [piste BE] map
el mar sea
marcar v dial
mareado dizzy
el mareo motion [travel BE] sickness
el marido husband
marrón brown
el martillo hammer
más more; **~ alto** louder; **~ bajo** lower; **~ barato** cheaper; **~ despacio** slower; **~ grande** larger; **~ pequeño** smaller; **~ rápido** faster; **~ tarde** later; **~ temprano** earlier
el masaje massage; **~ deportivo** sports massage
el mástil tent pole
el mecánico mechanic
el mechero lighter
la media hora half hour
mediano medium (size)
la medianoche midnight
el medicamento medicine

el médico doctor
medio half; **~ kilo** half-kilo; **~día** noon [midday BE]
medir v measure (someone)
mejor best
menos less
el mensaje message; **~ instantáneo** instant message
el mercado market
el mes month
la mesa table
el metro subway [underground BE]
el metro cuadrado square meter
la mezquita mosque
el microondas microwave
el minibar mini-bar
el minuto minute
el mirador overlook [viewpoint BE] (scenic place)
mirar v look
la misa mass (church service)
mismo same
los mocasines loafers
la mochila backpack
molestar v bother
la moneda coin, currency
mono cute
la montaña n mountain
el monumento conmemorativo memorial (place)
morado purple

el mostrador de información information desk

mostrar v display

la moto acuática jet ski

la motocicleta motorcycle

movilidad mobility

la mujer wife, woman

la multa fine (fee for breaking law)

la muñeca doll; ~ wrist

el músculo muscle

el museo museum

la música music; ~ **clásica** classical music; ~ **folk** folk music; ~ **pop** pop music

el muslo thigh

N

nacional domestic

la nacionalidad nationality

nada nothing

nadar v swim

las nalgas buttocks

naranja orange (color)

la nariz nose

necesitar v need

los negocios business

negro black

nevado snowy

la nevera refrigerator

el nieto grandchild

la niña girl

el niño boy, child

el nivel intermedio intermediate

no no

la noche evening,

night

el nombre name; ~ **de usuario** user-name

normal regular

las normas de vestuario dress code

el norte north

la novia girlfriend

el novio boyfriend

el número number; ~ **de fax** fax number; ~ **de permiso de conducir** driver's license number; ~ **de teléfono** phone number; ~ **de teléfono de información** information (phone)

O

la obra de teatro n play (theater)

el oculista optician

el oeste west

la oficina office; ~ **de correos** post office; ~ **de objetos perdidos** lost and found; ~ **de turismo** tourist information office

el ojo eye

la olla pot

la ópera opera

el ordenador computer

la oreja ear

la orina urine

el oro gold; ~ **amarillo** yellow gold; ~ **blanco** white gold

la orquesta orchestra

oscuro dark

el otro camino alternate route

la oxigenoterapia oxygen treatment

P

padecer del corazón heart condition

el padre father

pagar v pay

el pájaro bird

el palacio palace; ~ **de las cortes** parliament building

los palillos chinos chopsticks

la panadería bakery

los pantalones pants [trousers BE]; ~ **cortos** shorts

el pañal diaper [nappy BE]

el pañuelo de paper tissue

el papel paper; ~ **de aluminio** aluminum [kitchen BE] foil; ~ **de cocina** paper towel; ~ **higiénico** toilet paper

el paquete package

para for; ~ **llevar** to go [take away BE]; ~ **no fumadores** non-smoking

el paracetamol acetaminophen [paracetamol BE]

la parada n stop; ~ **de autobús** bus stop

el paraguas umbrella

pararse v stop

el párking parking garage

el parque playpen; ~ **park**; **de atracciones** amusement park

el partido game; ~ **de fútbol** soccer [football BE]; ~ **de voleibol** volleyball game

el pasajero passenger; ~ **con billete** ticketed passenger

el pasaporte passport

el pase de acceso a los remontes lift pass

el pasillo aisle

la pasta de dientes toothpaste

la pastelería pastry shop

el patio de recreo playground

el peatón pedestrian

el pecho chest (body part)

el pediatra pediatrician

la pedicura pedicure

pedir v order

el peinado hairstyle

el peine comb

la película movie

peligroso dangerous

el pelo hair

el peltre pewter

la peluquería de caballeros barber

la peluquería hair

salon
los pendientes earrings
el pene penis
la penicilina penicillin
la pensión bed and breakfast
pequeño small
perder v lose (something)
perdido lost
el perfume perfume
el periódico newspaper
la perla pearl
permitir v allow, permit
el perro guía guide dog
la persona con discapacidad visual visually impaired person
la picadura de insecto insect bite
picante spicy
picar v stamp (a ticket)
el pie foot
la piel skin
la pierna leg
la pieza part (for car)
los pijamas pajamas
la pila battery
la píldora Pill (birth control)
la piscina pool; **~ cubierta** indoor pool; **~ exterior** outdoor pool; **~ infantil** kiddie [paddling BE] pool
la pista trail [piste BE]

la pizzería pizzeria
el placer pleasure
la plancha n iron (clothes)
planchar v iron
la planta floor [storey BE]; **~ baja** ground floor
la plata silver; **~ esterlina** sterling silver
el platino platinum
el plato dish (kitchen); **~ principal** main course
la playa beach
la plaza town square
la policía police
la pomada cream (ointment)
ponerse en contacto con v contact
por for; **~** per; **~ día** per day; **~ favor** please; **~ hora** per hour; **~ la noche** overnight; **~ noche** per night; **~ semana** per week
el postre dessert
el precio price
precioso beautiful
el prefijo area code
la pregunta question
presentar v introduce
el preservativo condom
la primera clase first class
primero first
los principales sitios de interés main attraction
principiante beginner,

novice (skill level)
la prioridad de paso right of way
la prisa rush
el probador fitting room
probar v taste
el problema problem
el producto good; **~ de limpieza** cleaning product
programar v schedule
prohibir v prohibit
el pronóstico forecast
pronunciar v pronounce
el protector solar sunscreen
provisional temporary
próximo next
el público public
el pueblo village
el puente bridge
la puerta gate (airport); **~** door; **~ de incendios** fire door
el pulmón lung
la pulsera bracelet
el puro cigar

Q

qué what (question)
quedar bien v fit (clothing)
quedarse v stay
la queja complaint
la quemadura solar sunburn
querer v love (someone)
quién who (question)
el quiosco newsstand

R

la ración portion; **~ para niños** children's portion
la rampa para silla de ruedas wheelchair ramp
el rap rap (music)
rápido express, fast
la raqueta racket (sports); **~ de nieve** snowshoe
la reacción alérgica allergic reaction
recargar v recharge
la recepción reception
la receta prescription
recetar v prescribe
rechazar v decline (credit card)
recibir v receive
el recibo receipt
reciclar recycling
recoger v pick up (something)
la recogida de equipajes baggage claim
la recomendación recommendation
recomendar v recommend
el recorrido tour; **~ en autobús** bus tour; **~ turístico** sightseeing tour
recto straight
el recuerdo souvenir
el regalo gift
la región region
el registro check-in (hotel); **~ del coche** vehicle registration

la regla period (menstrual)

el Reino Unido United Kingdom (U.K.)

la relación relationship

rellenar *v* fill out (form)

el reloj watch; **~ de pared** wall clock

el remolque trailer

reparar *v* fix (repair)

el repelente de insectos insect repellent

repetir *v* repeat

la resaca hangover

la reserva reservation; **~ natural** nature preserve

reservar *v* reserve

el/la residente de la UE EU resident

respirar *v* breathe

el restaurante restaurant

retirar *v* withdraw; **~ fondos** withdrawal (bank)

retrasarse *v* delay

la reunión meeting

revelar *v* develop (film)

revisar *v* check (on something)

la revista magazine

el riñón kidney (body part)

el río river

robado stolen

robar *v* steal

el robo theft

la rodilla knee

rojo red

romántico romantic

romper *v* break

la ropa clothing; **~ interior** underwear

rosa pink

roto broken

el rugby rugby

la rueda tire [tyre BE]; **~ pinchada** flat tire [tyre BE]

las ruinas ruins

la ruta route; **~ de senderismo** walking route

S

la sábana sheet

el sacacorchos corkscrew

el saco de dormir sleeping bag

la sala room; **~ de conciertos** concert hall; **~ de espera** waiting room; **~ de reuniones** meeting room

la salida check-out (hotel)

la salida *n* exit; **~ de urgencia** emergency exit

las salidas departures (airport)

salir *v* exit, leave

el salón room; **~ de congresos** convention hall; **~ de juegos recreativos** arcade; **~ de manicura** nail salon

¡Salud! Cheers!

la salud health

las sandalias sandals

sangrar *v* bleed

la sangre blood

el santuario shrine

la sartén frying pan

la sauna sauna

el secador de pelo hair dryer

la secreción discharge (bodily fluid)

la seda silk

sediento thirsty

la seguridad security

el seguro insurance

seguro safe (protected)

el sello *n* stamp (postage)

el semáforo traffic light

la semana week

semanal weekly

el seminario seminar

el sendero trail; **~ para bicicletas** bike route

el seno breast

sentarse *v* sit

separado separated (marriage)

ser *v* be

serio serious

el servicio restroom [toilet BE]; **~ service** (in a restaurant); **~ completo** full-service; **~ de habitaciones** room service; **~**

inalámbrico a internet wireless internet service; **~ de internet** internet service; **~ de lavandería** laundry

service; **~ de limpieza de habitaciones** housekeeping service

la servilleta napkin

sí yes

el sida AIDS

la silla chair; **~ para niños** child seat; **~ de ruedas** wheelchair

el símbolo symbol (keyboard)

sin without; **~ alcohol** non-alcoholic; **~ grasa** fat free; **~ receta** over the counter (medication)

la sinagoga synagogue

el sitio de interés attraction (place)

el sobre envelope

el socorrista lifeguard

el sol sun

solamente only

soleado sunny

solo alone

soltero single (marriage)

el sombrero hat

la somnolencia drowsiness

sordo deaf

soso bland

el suavizante conditioner

el subtítulo subtitle

sucio dirty

la sudadera sweatshirt

el suelo floor

el sujetador bra

súper super (fuel)

superior upper
el supermercado grocery store, supermarket
la supervisión supervision
el sur south
el surfista windsurfer

T

la tabla board; ~ **de snowboard** snowboard; ~ **de surf** surfboard
la talla size; ~ **grande** plus size; ~ **pequeña** petite size
el taller garage (repair)
el talón de equipaje luggage [baggage BE] ticket
el tampón tampon
la taquilla locker; ~ **reservation desk**
tarde late (time)
la tarde afternoon
la tarjeta card; ~ **de cajero automático** ATM card; ~ **de crédito** credit card; ~ **de débito** debit card; ~ **de embarque** boarding pass; ~ **internacional de estudiante** international student card; ~ **de memoria** memory card; ~ **de negocios** business card; ~ **postal** postcard; ~ **de seguro** insurance card; ~ **de socio** membership card; ~ **telefónica** phone card
la tasa fee
el taxi taxi
la taza cup; ~ **medidora** measuring cup
el teatro theater; ~ **de la ópera** opera house
la tela impermeable groundcloth [groundsheet BE]
el teleférico cable car
el teléfono telephone; ~ **móvil** cell [mobile BE] phone; ~ **público** pay phone
la telesilla chair lift
el telesquí ski/drag lift
la televisión TV
el templo temple (religious)
temprano early
el tenedor fork
tener v have; ~ **dolor** v hurt (have pain); ~ **náuseas** v be nauseous
el tenis tennis
la tensión arterial blood pressure
la terminal terminal (airport)
terminar v end
la terracotta terracotta
terrible terrible
el texto n text (message)
el tiempo time;

~ **weather**
la tienda store; ~ **de alimentos naturales** health food store; ~ **de antigüedades** antique store; ~ **de bebidas alcohólicas** liquor store [off-licence BE]; ~ **de campaña** tent; ~ **de deportes** sporting goods store; ~ **de fotografía** camera store; ~ **de juguetes** toy store; ~ **de música** music store; ~ **de recuerdos** souvenir store; ~ **de regalos** gift shop; ~ **de ropa** clothing store
las tijeras scissors
la tintorería dry cleaner
el tipo de cambio exchange rate
tirar v pull (door sign)
la tirita bandage
la toalla towel
la toallita baby wipe
el tobillo ankle
el torneo de golf golf tournament
la torre tower
la tos n cough
toser v cough
el total total (amount)
trabajar v work
tradicional traditional
traducir v translate
traer v bring
tragar v swallow

el traje suit
tranquilo quiet
el tren train; ~ **rápido** express train
triste sad
la trona highchair
el trozo piece
la tumbona deck chair
el turista tourist

U

último last
la universidad university
uno one
la uña nail; ~ **del dedo** fingernail; ~ **del pie** toenail
urgente urgent
usar v use

V

las vacaciones vacation [holiday BE]
vaciar v empty
la vacuna vaccination
la vagina vagina
la validez valid
valioso valuable
el valle valley
el valor value
el vaquero denim
los vaqueros jeans
el vaso glass (drinking)
el váter químico chemical toilet
vegetariano vegetarian
la vejiga bladder
vender v sell
el veneno poison
venir v come

la ventana window
el ventilador fan (appliance)
ver *v* see
verde green
el vestido dress (piece of clothing)
el viaje trip
el vidrio glass (material)
viejo old

la viña vineyard
la violación *n* rape
violar *v* rape
el visado visa (passport document)
visitar *v* visit
la vitamina vitamin
la vitrina display case
viudo widowed
vivir *v* live

vomitar *v* vomit
el vuelo flight; ~ **internacional** international flight; ~ **nacional** domestic flight

Z

la zapatería shoe store
las zapatillas slippers; ~ **de deporte** sneaker
los zapatos shoes
la zona area; ~ **de compras** shopping area; ~ **de fumadores** smoking area; ~ **para picnic** picnic area
el zoológico zoo
zurcir *v* mend

INDEX

Berlitz pocket guide

MADRID

Seventh Edition 2019

Editor: Helen Fanthorpe
Updater: Magdalena Helsztyńska-Stadnik
Author: Neil Schlecht and Vicky Hayward
Head of DTP and Pre-Press: Rebeka Davies
Managing Editor: Carine Tracanelli
Picture Editor: Tom Smyth
Cartography Update: Carte
Update Production: Apa Digital
Photography Credits: Alamy 1, 51; AP/REX/
Shutterstock 21; Bigstock 30; Corbis 5TC;
Corrie Wingate/Apa Publications 4TC, 4TL,
33, 38, 71, 92; Dreamstime 63, 65; Getty
Images 4ML, 5M, 12, 47, 68, 88, 96, 100,
102; iStock 5MC, 7, 7R, 11, 14, 28, 31, 32,
35, 37, 39, 41, 53, 54, 61, 74, 77, 81, 84, 104;
Public domain 5T, 17, 18, 23, 44, 45; Robert
B. Fishman/Picfair 43; Shutterstock 4MC,
5MC, 5M, 6L, 6R, 26, 48, 55, 56, 58, 67, 72,
78, 83, 87, 91, 95, 105
Cover Picture: Riccardo Spila/4Corners
Images

Distribution
UK, Ireland and Europe: Apa Publications
(UK) Ltd; sales@insightguides.com
United States and Canada: Ingram
Publisher Services; ips@ingramcontent.com
Australia and New Zealand: Woodslane;
info@woodslane.com.au
Southeast Asia: Apa Publications (SN) Pte;
singaporeoffice@insightguides.com
Worldwide: Apa Publications (UK) Ltd;
sales@insightguides.com

**Special Sales, Content Licensing
and CoPublishing**
Insight Guides can be purchased in bulk
quantities at discounted prices. We can
create special editions, personalised jackets
and corporate imprints tailored to your
needs. sales@insightguides.com;
www.insightguides.biz

Contact us
Every effort has been made to provide
accurate information in this publication,
but changes are inevitable. The publisher
cannot be responsible for any resulting loss,
inconvenience or injury. We would appreciate
it if readers would call our attention to any
errors or outdated information. We also
welcome your suggestions; please contact
us at: berlitz@apaguide.co.uk
www.insightguides.com/berlitz

RED DE METRO Y METRO LIGERO *Metro and Light Rail Network*

SIMBOLOGÍA - Key

- Estación accesible / ascensor — *Step-free access / lift*
- Transbordo corto — *Metro interchange*
- Transbordo largo — *Metro interchange with long walking distance*
- Cambio de tren — *Change of trains*
- Circular
- Metro Ligero — *Light Rail*
- Cercanías — *Suburban railway*
- Autobuses interurbanos — *Suburban buses*
- Autobuses largo recorrido nocturno — *Night bus line terminal*
- Terminal Autobuses nocturnos — *Night bus line terminal*
- Autobús Exprés Aeropuerto — *Airport Express Bus*
- Estación de tren — *Railway station*

- Aeropuerto / *Airport* Adolfo Suárez Madrid-Barajas
- Zonas tarifarias — *Fare zones*
- ATENCIÓN A LA TARIFA — Validación a la SALIDA — *PAY THE RIGHT FARE — Ticket checked at the EXIT*
- Oficina de gestión tarjeta transporte público — *Public Transport Card Office*
- Centro de información — *Customer Service*
- Objetos perdidos — *Lost and found*

- Biblioteca metro — *Metro Library*
- Productos Oficiales Metro — *Official Metro merchandising*
- Aparcamiento disuasorio gratuito — *Free Park and Ride*
- Aparcamiento disuasorio de pago — *Paid Park and Ride*
- Estacionamiento de bicicletas — *Bicycle parking*
- Espacio Histórico de Metro — *Historic Space of Metro*

Líneas

1. Pinar de Chamartín — Valdecarros
2. Las Rosas — Cuatro Caminos
3. Villaverde Alto — Moncloa
4. Argüelles — Pinar de Chamartín — Alameda de Osuna — Casa de Campo
6. Circular
7. Hospital del Henares — Pitis
8. Nuevos Ministerios — Aeropuerto
9. Paco de Lucía — Arganda del Rey — Hospital Infanta Sofía — Puerta del Sur
10. La Fortuna — Plaza Elíptica
11. MetroSur
12.
R. Opera — Príncipe Pío

- ML1. Pinar de Chamartín — Las Tablas
- ML2. Colonia Jardín — Estación de Aravaca
- ML3. Colonia Jardín — Puerta de Boadilla

www.metromadrid.es
Síguenos en / *Follow us on*

Comunidad de Madrid

CONSORCIO TRANSPORTES MADRID

Metro

Berlitz®

speaking your language

phrase book & dictionary
phrase book & CD

Available in: Arabic, Brazilian Portuguese*, Burmese*, Cantonese Chinese, Croatian, Czech*, Danish*, Dutch, English, Filipino, Finnish*, French, German, Greek, Hebrew*, Hindi*, Hungarian*, Indonesian, Italian, Japanese, Korean, Latin American Spanish, Malay, Mandarin Chinese, Mexican Spanish, Norwegian, Polish, Portuguese, Romanian*, Russian, Spanish, Swedish, Thai, Turkish, Vietnamese
*Book only

www.berlitzpublishing.com